KETO DESSERTS COOKBOOK

Best Low Carb, High-Fat Treats that'll Satisfy Your Sweet Tooth, Boost Energy And Reverse Disease

Francis Michael

COPYRIGHT © 2020 by Francis Michael

ISBN: 978-1-952504-10-5

All rights reserved. This book is copyright protected and it's for personal use only. Without the prior written permission of the publisher, no part of this publication should be reproduced, distributed, or transmitted in any form or by any means, including photocopying, recording, or other electronic or mechanical methods. This publication is sold with the idea that the publisher is not required to render accounting, officially permitted, or otherwise, qualified services. Seek for the services of a legal or professional, a practiced individual in the profession if advice is needed.

DISCLAIMER

The information contained in this book is geared for educational and entertainment purposes only. Strenuous efforts have been made towards providing accurate, up to date and reliable complete information. The information in this book is true and complete to the best of our knowledge. Neither the publisher nor the author takes any responsibility for any possible consequences of reading or enjoying the recipes in this book. The author and publisher disclaim any liability in connection with the use of information contained in this book. Under no circumstance will any legal responsibility or blame be apportioned against the author or publisher for any reparation, damages, or monetary loss due to the information herein, either directly or indirectly.

Table of Contents

INTRODUCTION 8

Ketogenic Desserts Basics 8

Benefits of Keto Desserts 9

CAKE 10

- Lemon Coconut Cake 10
- Birthday Cake Shake 11
- Chocolate Cake 12
- Vanilla Buttercream Cake 13
- Carrot Cake 14
- Zucchini Bundt Cake 16
- Italian Lemon Ricotta Cheesecake 17
- Lemon Poppy Seed Cake 19
- Vanilla Pound Cake 21
- Pumpkin Bundt Cake 22

COOKIES 24

- Peanut Butter Cookies 24
- Spice Cookies 25
- Pecan Snowball Cookies 26
- Gingersnap Cookies 27
- Chocolate Chip Cookies 28

Chewy Pecan Cookies 29

Pumpkin Cream Cheese Cookies 30

Chocolate Chip Cookies 31

Snickerdoodle Cookies 32

Chocolate Fudge Cookies 33

Shortbread Cookies 34

Flourless Chocolate Cookies 35

Soft n' Chewy Cookies 36

Chocolate Butter Cookies 37

BARS 38

Granola Bars 38

Nut Bars 40

Cookie Dough Bars 41

Chocolate Crunch Bars 42

Protein Bars 43

Almond Joy Bars 45

Chocolate Collagen Candy Bar 47

Lemon Bars 48

Snickers Bars 50

Peanut Butter Chocolate Bars 52

Magic Bars 53

Fathead Blueberry Bars 54

Cookie Bars 56

Chocolate Fudge Protein Bars 57

TARTS 58

Chocolate & Lime Tarts 58

Bakewell Tarts 60

Strawberry Tart 61

Chocolate Espresso Mini Tarts 62

Dough Tart 63

Chocolate Hazelnut Tart...64

Butter Tarts 65

Tart Crust 66

Cheesecake Tarts 67

Toasted Cream Tarts 69

PIES 71

Sweet Pie Crust 71

Lemon Meringue Pie 72

Samoa Pie..74

Mini Chicken Pot Pies...76

Greek Spinach Pie..78

Lemon Coconut Custard Pie 79

Chocolate Almond Butter Pie 80

Peppermint Cheesecake Pie...81

- Grasshopper Pie 83
- Almond Flour Pie 84
- Graham Cracker Pie 85

FROZEN DESSERTS 86

- Mint and Chocolate Chip Ice Bombs 86
- Strawberry-Basil Ice Cups 87
- Vanilla Ice Cream 88
- Shamrock Shake 89
- Peanut Butter Chocolate Ice Cream 90
- Butter Pecan Ice Cream 91
- Peanut Butter Cup Milkshake 92
- Strawberry Homemade Ice Cream 93

MOUSSE & CUSTARD 94

- Chocolate Mousse 94
- Peanut Butter Mousse 95
- Vanilla Custard 96
- Crème Anglaise Custard 97
- Caramel Mousse 98
- Chocolate Custard 99
- Pumpkin Cheesecake Mousse 100
- Almond Milk Custard 101
- Egg Custard 102

Pumpkin Custard 103

CANDY & CONFECTIONS 104

Chocolate Coconut Fat Bombs 104

Butterscotch Candy 105

Lemon Drop Gummies 106

Vanilla Fat Bombs 107

Peppermint Frost Breath Mints 108

Lemon Curd 109

INTRODUCTION

Ketogenic Desserts Basics

One great thing about the ketogenic diet is that, it doesn't make me try to neglect my sweet tooth. Keto desserts are always around to save the day. When your body enters ketosis, you will observe that your desire for sweets disappears.

If you've been eating sweet your whole life, something will definitely make you crave to eat some sweets. And that's alright!

On keto, there are lots of decadent desserts that are easy to make and equally satisfy your sweet tooth cravings. You don't have to eat healthy by sticking to fruits for dessert alone. Majority of fruits are negative when it comes to the keto diet. There are so many different keto recipes that can serve as substitute for your desired dessert and it won't knock you out of ketosis.

The goal and aim of this cookbook is to find easy to make desserts. Sometimes you just don't have the luxury of time to wait in making your desserts and do not require you sticking your hands into an oven.

Yes, these are completely no-bake recipes.

So we went ahead and made over **100+** decadent desserts that are both low in carbs and high in fats. You check with your doctor if you have diabetes, hypoglycemia, or heart disease if you're interested in starting the keto diet.

Benefits of Keto Desserts

1. **Aids in Weight Loss:**

It takes more work to turn fat into energy because ketogenic diet can help speed up weight loss. Ketogenic diet does not leave you hungry because the diet is high in protein. It helps to speed up weight loss.

2. **Reduces Acne:**

There are different causes of acne, and they may be related to diet and blood sugar. Eating a diet high in processed and refined carbohydrates can affect gut bacteria which lead to blood sugar fluctuations and may have influence on skin health. Reducing carb intake could reduce some cases of acne.

3. **May Help Reduce Risk of Cancer:**

Scientific research has proven that ketogenic diet may help prevent or even treat certain cancers. It may be a suitable complementary treatment to chemotherapy and radiation in people living with cancer because it causes more oxidative stress in cancer cells than in normal cells. Ketogenic diet reduces high blood sugar, and insulin complications, which may be related with some cancers.

4. **Improves Heart Health:**

Once the ketogenic diet is followed in an appropriate manner, the diet can improve heart health by reducing cholesterol.

5. **May Protect Brain Functioning:**

Ketogenic diet offers neuroprotective benefits which may help treat or prevent conditions like Parkinson's, Alzheimer's, and even some sleep disorders. Scientific studies has also found that children placed on a ketogenic diet had improved alertness and cognitive functioning.

6. **Potentially Reduces Seizures:**

A complete combination of fat, protein, and carbs alters the way the body uses energy, resulting in ketosis. Ketosis always results when there's increase level of ketone bodies in the blood. It can lead to a reduction in seizures in people with epilepsy.

CAKE

Lemon Coconut Cake

Preparation time: 10 minutes

Cook time: 45 minutes

Total time: 55 minutes

Servings: 10 Slices

Ingredients:

Coconut Cake ingredients:

- ½ Cup of Coconut Flour 40g / 1.2 ounces
- 5 Eggs
- ¼ Cup of Erythritol (SoNourished) 30g / 1 ounces
- ½ Cup of Butter, melted 125g / 4 ounces
- ½ Lemon, Juiced
- ½ Teaspoon of Lemon Zest
- ½ Teaspoon of xanthan gum
- ½ Teaspoon of Salt

Icing Ingredients:

- 1 Cup of Cream Cheese 225g / 8 ounces
- 3 Tablespoon of Powdered Erythritol (SoNourished)
- 1 Teaspoon of Vanilla Extract
- ½ Teaspoon of Lemon Zest

Cooking Instructions:

1. Add the egg whites and yolks into separate bowl. Beat the egg whites to form white peaks. Add the remaining cake ingredients and the egg yolks into the bowl.

2. Give everything a good mix until well combined. Add the mixture into a greased loaf tin (9" X 5"). Bake at 180° C (355° F) for 45 minutes.

3. Beat together the cream cheese, erythritol, vanilla extract and lemon zest with an electric beater. Set aside and ice the cake when it has done cooking.

4. Slice and enjoy

Nutrition Facts

Calories 145 Kcal | Total Fat 12g | Total Carbohydrates 1g | Protein 4g

Birthday Cake Shake

Preparation time: 5 minutes

Cook time: 1 minute

Total time: 6 minutes

Serves: 2 Cups

Ingredients:

- ¼ Cup of unsweetened vanilla almond milk (60ml)
- ¼ Cup of non-fat Greek yogurt (55g)
- ¼ Cup of oatmeal (20g)
- 1½ Scoops vanilla whey protein powder (45g)
- 1½ Tablespoon of sugar substitute (18g)
- 1 Teaspoon of Sprinkles (3g)
- 1 Cup of Ice (135g)

Cooking Instructions:

1. Add together all the ingredients into your blender.
2. Blend the ingredients until smooth.
3. Serve and enjoy!

Nutrition Facts

Amounts per Serving

Calories: 361 Kcal | Fat: 3g | Carbohydrates: 39g | Protein: 45g

Chocolate Cake

Preparation time: 10 minutes

Cook time: 30 minutes

Total time: 40 minutes

Servings: 12

Ingredients:

- 300 g / 10.5 ounces unsweetened chocolate
- 300 g / 10.5 ounces butter unsalted (1 1/3 cup melted)
- 6 eggs
- ½ cup / 50g of almond flour or ground almonds
- 1 ½ cup / 150g of powdered erythritol
- Dash of salt

Cooking Instructions:

1. Pre-heat the oven to 170°C / 340°F. Add the butter and chocolate in the microwave to melt, then stir to dissolve. Set aside.

2. In a medium bowl, beat the eggs until foamy. Add the sweetener and give everything a good mix.

3. Add together the melted chocolate and butter with the almond flour. Give everything a good stir with a spoon until just combined.

4. Arrange the bottom of a 20 cm / 8 inch spring form with parchment paper and grease the sides of the spring form pan with butter. Add the cake batter.

5. Bake for about 30 minutes on the center shelf until the top of the cake is firm in the center. Allow to cool before removing from the cake tin.

6. Dust the cake with cocoa powder. Serve and enjoy!

Nutrition Facts

Amount per Serving

Calories 389 Kcal | Fat 37.8g | Carbohydrates 3g | Protein 8.1g

Vanilla Buttercream Cake

Preparation time: 15 minutes

Cook time: 25 minutes

Total time: 40 minutes

Serves: 6

Ingredients:

- 4 oz. of Stevia sweetened dark chocolate, chopped
- ½ cup of coconut cream
- 2 eggs
- 30 drops liquid stevia
- 2 tbsp. of cacao powder
- ½ cup of almond flour
- 2 tsp. of baking soda
- ¼ tsp. of fine salt
- ½ lb. of Kerry gold butter (1 block), softened.
- 3 scoops Perfect Keto Vanilla Collagen MCT or MCT powder
- Chocolate Chips or Cacao nibs

Cooking Instructions:

1. Pre-heat the oven to 350°F. Microwave the chopped chocolate for 30-40 seconds until soft. Whisk until smooth.

2. Add in the coconut cream and whisk everything until smooth. Once it has cooled, mix together the eggs and stevia until combined. Set aside.

3. In a separate bowl, mix together all of the dry ingredients and fold them into the wet mix. Add the batter to a greased loaf pan. Bake for 25-30 minutes.

4. Allow the cake to cool before removing from the pan. Cut the loaf in the middle with a knife. Whip the butter and Vanilla MCT powder until smooth.

5. Put 2 tbsp. to one square, and smooth it out. Stack the two cake squares. Add one thin coat of butter cream, and refrigerate for about 20 minutes to harden.

6. Remove from the freezer and add the buttercream with a spatula. Garnish with chocolate chips. Serve and enjoy!

Nutrition Facts

Calories: 623 Kcal | Fat: 61g | Carbohydrates: 8g | Protein: 10g

Carrot Cake

Hands-on: 10 minutes

Total time: 1 hour 10 minutes

Servings: 16

Ingredients:

Cake Ingredients:

- 2 ¾ cups of almond flour
- 1 ¼ cups of powdered Erythritol or Swerve
- 2 teaspoons of gluten-free baking powder
- 2 teaspoons of cinnamon
- ½ teaspoon of sea salt
- 6 large eggs
- ½ cup of melted butter or ghee
- ¼ cup of unsweetened almond milk
- 2 cups grated carrots
- 2 teaspoons of sugar-free vanilla extract
- ½ cup of pecan pieces

Frosting:

- 1 cup of full-fat cream cheese
- 1 cup of powdered Erythritol or Swerve
- 1/3 cup of heavy whipping cream
- ½ cup of pecan pieces, divided

Cooking Instructions:

1. Preheat the oven to 160°C/ 325°F. Line a parchment paper a round 23 cm/ 9 inch. In a medium bowl, mix together the dry cake ingredients except for the carrots and pecans.

2. Add in the wet ingredients and give everything a good stir until smooth. Add in the carrots and pecans and stir. Pour the batter into the prepared pan.

3. Bake for 45-60 minutes or until a toothpick inserted into the middle comes out clean. Remove the cake from oven and allow to cool for a couple of minutes.

To Make the Frosting:

1. Cream together the cream cheese and whipping cream with a hand mixer until smooth. Add in the powdered Swerve and beat everything until combined.

2. If the frosting is too thick, add in another 2-3 tbsp. of cream, one at a time, until your desire consistency is achieved. Stir in half of the pecan pieces.

3. Then, frost the cake with the icing using a spoon or offset spatula. Sprinkle the rest of the pecans over the top.

4. Serve immediately and enjoy! Store covered and chilled for up to 7 days.

Nutrition Facts

Amounts per Serving

Calories: 295 Kcal | Carbohydrate: 4.9 g | Protein 8 g | Fat 27.7 g

Zucchini Bundt Cake

Hands-on time: 10 minutes

Total time: 1 hour 10 minutes

Serving: 16 slices

Ingredients:

Cake Ingredients:

- 2 ¾ cups of almond flour (275 g)
- 1 1/3 cups of powdered Erythritol or Swerve (200 g)
- ½ cup of cacao powder (43 g)
- 2 teaspoons of gluten-free baking powder
- ½ teaspoon of sea salt or pink Himalayan salt
- 6 large eggs
- ½ cup of melted butter or ghee (4 ounces)
- 2 medium zucchini, pureed (8.5 ounces)
- 2 teaspoons of sugar-free vanilla extract

Frosting Ingredients:

- ¼ cup of virgin coconut oil (1.9 ounces)
- ½ cup of cacao powder (1.5 ounces)
- Stevia drops, to taste

Cooking Instructions:

1. Preheat the oven to 165°C/ 325°F. Coat a Bundt pan with oil. In two different bowls, mix together the wet and dry ingredients.

2. Add the wet mixture into the dry mixture and give everything a good mix. Pour the batter into the Bundt pan. Smooth out the top.

3. Place to the oven and bake for 60 minutes or until a toothpick inserted into the middle comes out clean. Allow the cake to cool before removing onto a cake stand.

To Make the Frosting:

1. Melt together the coconut oil and cacao powder. Put the stevia to taste 2-3 drops at a time. Add the frosting over the cake and serve. Store covered for up to 4 days.

Nutrition Facts

Amounts per Serving

Calories: 229 Kcal | Carbohydrates 3.8 g | Protein 7.3 g | Fat 20.7 g

Italian Lemon Ricotta Cheesecake

Preparation time: 10 minutes

Cook time: 15 minutes

Total time: 25 minutes

Servings: 16

Ingredients:

Crust ingredients:

- 2 cups of almond flour
- 6 tablespoons of unsalted butter
- ¼ teaspoon of sea salt
- 2 tablespoons of low carb sweetener

Filling Ingredients:

- 16 oz. of cream cheese, softened
- 15 oz. of ricotta cheese
- 1 cup of low carb sweetener
- 1 tablespoon of vanilla extract
- 2 teaspoons of fresh lemon zest
- ½ teaspoon of lemon extract
- 1 ½ cups of heavy cream

Cooking Instructions:

1. Preheat the oven to 350°F. Add the butter in a microwave safe bowl and heat to melt.

2. In a medium bowl, combine together the melted butter, almond flour, sea salt, and sweetener.

3. Spray a non-stick cooking spray on a 9 inch glass pie pan. Pour the crust into the pan. Bake for 12-15 minutes. Remove the cake and allow to cool on a rack.

For the Filling:

1. In a stand mixer or medium bowl, combine together the cream cheese, ricotta cheese, sweetener, the lemon and vanilla extracts, and the lemon zest.

2. Blend the ingredients together on medium speed until the filling is creamy and smooth.

3. In a separate bowl, use the hand mixer to whip the heavy cream until stiff peaks form. Gently fold the whipped cream into the cream cheese mixture.

4. Pour the filling into the cooled crust and refrigerate for about 4 hours before serving. Serve and enjoy!

Nutrition Facts

Amount per Serving

Calories 339 Kcal | Carbohydrates 5g | Fat 32g | Protein 8g

Lemon Poppy Seed Cake

Preparation time: 15 minutes

Cook time: 1 hour

Total time: 1 hour 15 minutes

Servings: 16

Ingredients:

- ¾ cup of Butter, softened
- 1 cup of Erythritol
- 4 large Egg, at room temperature
- ¾ cup of Sour cream
- 2 tablespoons of Lemon extract
- 2 teaspoons of Vanilla extract, optional
- 3 cups of Blanched almond flour
- 2 teaspoons of Gluten-free baking powder
- 3 tablespoons of Poppy seeds
- ½ teaspoon of Sea salt

Lemon Glaze Ingredients:

- ¾ cup of Powdered erythritol
- ¼ cup of Lemon juice
- ¼ teaspoon of Vanilla extract, optional

Cooking Instructions:

1. Preheat the oven to 350°F/ 177°C. Grease a Bundt pan. In a medium bowl, beat together the butter and sweetener with a hand mixer until fluffy.

2. Then, beat in the eggs, sour cream, lemon extract and vanilla extract. In a separate bowl, add together the almond flour, baking powder, poppy seeds, and sea salt.

3. Give everything a good stir. Beat the dry ingredients into the wet mixture, about a cup at a time. Pour the batter to the Bundt pan and smooth the top.

4. Bake for about 40 minutes, or until the top turns golden brown. Continue baking for 20-35 minutes, or until a toothpick inserted in the middle comes out clean.

5. Allow to cool for about 15 minutes. Remove the cake onto a cooling rack.

To Make the Glaze:

1. In a medium bowl, whisk together the powdered sweetener, lemon juice and vanilla extract. Drizzle the mixture over the cake.

2. Serve and enjoy!

Nutrition Facts

Amount per Serving

Calories 248 Kcal | Fat 23g | Protein 7g | Total Carbs 6g

Vanilla Pound Cake

Preparation time: 10 minutes

Cook time: 50 minutes

Total time: 1 hour

Yield: 12 slices

Ingredients:

- 1 ½ cup of almond flour
- ¼ cup of coconut flour
- 2 scoops of Perfect Keto Vanilla Collagen Powder
- 1/3 cup of monk fruit or stevia powder
- 1 tsp. of baking powder
- ¼ tsp. of salt
- 3 large whole eggs
- 1 tsp. of vanilla extract
- ¼ cup of sour cream
- 1 cup of milk
- ¼ cup of melted butter

Cooking Instructions:

1. Preheat the oven to 350°F. Grease an 8×4 loaf pan with nonstick spray. Line the bottom of the pan with parchment paper.

2. In a medium bowl, add together the almond flour, coconut flour, collagen, baking powder, sweetener, and salt. Whisk everything to combine.

3. In a separate bowl, or stand mixer, add together the eggs and vanilla. Beat the mixture on high speed for 1 minute or until fluffy.

4. Add together the sour cream, melted butter, and milk. Beat on high speed for 30-45 seconds. Gently add the dry ingredients to wet ingredients in 2 batches.

5. Give everything a good mix to combine. Allow to rest for about 2 minutes and mix on low speed. Pour batter into the loaf pan.

6. Bake for 50-60 minutes until golden brown and a toothpick inserted in the middle comes out clean. Add additional baking time if desired.

Nutrition Facts

Calories: 175 Kcal | Fat: 15g | Carbohydrates: 5g | Protein: 7g

Pumpkin Bundt Cake

Hands-on time: 15 minutes

Total time: 1 hour 15 minutes

Servings: 12

Ingredients:

Cake Ingredients:

- 2 ¾ cups of almond flour (275 g)
- ½ cup of butter or ghee, melted (113 g)
- 1 1/3 cups of powdered Erythritol or Swerve (210 g)
- 6 large eggs
- 8.5 ounces of pumpkin puree (240 g)
- 2 teaspoons of sugar-free vanilla extract
- 2 teaspoons of pumpkin pie spice
- ½ teaspoon of salt
- 2 teaspoons of gluten-free baking powder
- Powdered Erythritol or Swerve for dusting, optional

Glaze Ingredients:

- ¼ cup of unsalted butter or ghee (56 g)
- ½ cup of powdered Erythritol or Swerve (80 g)
- 1 teaspoon of cinnamon
- 1 teaspoon of sugar-free vanilla extract

Cooking Instructions

1. Preheat the oven to 160°C/ 325°F. In a medium bowl, add together the dry ingredients and give everything a good stir to combine.

2. Add in the eggs, pumpkin puree, vanilla extract and melted butter. Combine everything with a hand mixer or stand mixer until smooth.

3. Pour the batter into a greased Bundt pan. Place to the oven and bake for 60 minutes. Bake the cake until a toothpick inserted into the middle comes out clean.

4. Allow to cool for 15 minutes before removing onto a cooling rack.

To Make the Glaze:

1. Add all the glaze ingredients in a small pot and cook over low heat. Cook just until melted. Add the glaze over the Bundt cake.

2. Dust the cake with powdered Erythritol or Swerve. Allow to cool down before slicing. Serve and enjoy!

3. Store at room temperature for up to 2 days, or refrigerate for up to 5 days.

Nutritional Facts

Amounts per Serving

Calories: 289 Kcal | Carbohydrate: 4.8 g | Protein: 8.4 g | Fat: 26 grams

COOKIES

Peanut Butter Cookies

Preparation time: 15 minutes

Cook time: 20 minutes

Total time: 35 minutes

Servings: 7

Ingredients:

- ¾ cup of No Sugar Peanut butter
- 2/3 cup of Powdered Erythritol
- 1 Large Egg
- ½ Teaspoon of Vanilla Extract
- ½ Teaspoon of Salt
- ¼ Cup of Butter

Cooking Instructions:

1. Preheat the oven to 355°F (180°C). Melt the butter. In a medium bowl, mix together all of the ingredients until well combined.

2. Fold them into 7 balls and make the top flat with a fork. Bake for 15 – 20 minutes or until they begin to turn brown.

3. Allow the cake to cool for about 20 minutes. Remove the cake and place onto a baking tray. Slice and serve!

Nutrition Facts

Amounts per Serving

Calories: 217kcal | Carbohydrates: 5g | Protein: 8g | Fat: 19g

Spice Cookies

Preparation time: 10 minutes

Cook time: 15 minutes

Total time: 25 minutes

Servings: 18 Cookies

Ingredients:

Cream Together

- 4 tablespoons of softened butter or coconut oil
- 2 tablespoons of agave nectar
- 1 egg
- 2 tbsp. of water

Add Dry Ingredients

- 1 cup of Almond Flour
- 1/3 cup of Truvia or ½ cup of sugar
- 2 Teaspoons of ground ginger
- 1 Teaspoon of ground cinnamon
- ½ Teaspoon of Ground Nutmeg
- 1 Teaspoon of Baking Soda
- ¼ Teaspoon of Salt

Cooking Instructions:

1. Preheat the oven to 350°F. Line a Bundt pan with parchment paper and set aside. Cream together the butter, agave nectar, egg, and water with a hand mixer.

2. Add all the dry ingredients to the wet and mix everything on low speed. Fold them into 2 teaspoons of balls and line on a baking tray with parchment paper.

3. Bake for 12-15 minutes or until the top turns lightly browned. Remove from the heat and allow to cool for a couple of minutes.

4. Serve and enjoy! Store in an air-tight container.

Nutrition Facts

Amounts per Serving

Calories: 122kcal | Fat: 10g | Carbohydrates: 5g | Protein: 3g

Pecan Snowball Cookies

Preparation time: 5 minutes

Cook time: 15 minutes

Total time: 20 minutes

Servings: 24

Ingredients:

- 8 tablespoons of Ghee or butter
- 1 ½ cup of almond flour (150 g)
- 1 cup of pecans 120 grams, chopped
- ½ cup of Swerve Confectioners Sweetener (78 g)
- 1 teaspoon of vanilla extract
- ½ teaspoon of vanilla liquid stevia
- ¼ teaspoon of salt
- Extra confectioners to roll balls in

Cooking Instructions:

1. Preheat the oven to 350°F. Add together all of the ingredients into food processor and process until batter forms a ball.

2. Taste and adjust the batter with sweetener if desired. Line a baking sheet with parchment paper. Make 24 mounds with a cookie scoop.

3. Fold each mound with your hands. Refrigerate for 20-30 minutes. Bake in the oven for 15 minutes or until golden. Allow the cake to cool for a couple of minutes.

4. Once the cake has completely cooled, roll each in some confectioner's sweetener. Store in an air tight container. Serve and enjoy!

Nutrition Facts

Amount per Serving

Calories 112Kcal | Fat 11g | Carbohydrates 2g | Protein 1g

Gingersnap Cookies

Yields: 24

Ingredients:

- 2 cups of almond flour
- ¼ cup of unsalted butter
- 1 cup of erythritol
- 1 large egg
- 1 teaspoon of vanilla extract
- ¼ teaspoon of salt
- 2 teaspoons of ground ginger
- ¼ teaspoon of ground nutmeg
- ¼ teaspoon of ground cloves
- ½ teaspoon of ground cinnamon

Cooking Ingredients:

1. Preheat the oven to 350°F. In a medium bowl, mix together all the dry ingredients.

2. In a separate bowl, mix together the melted unsalted butter, egg, and vanilla extract until well combined. Pour the wet ingredients to the dry ingredients.

3. Blend everything with a hand mixer until combined. Measure out each cookie with a tablespoon. Flatten the top of each cookie with a spatula.

4. Bake for 10-12 minutes or until the edges begins to turn brown. Allow to cool for a couple of minutes. Serve and enjoy!

Nutrition Facts

Amounts per Serving

Calories: 77.88 Kcal | Fats: 7.13g | Carbohydrates: 0.81g | Protein: 2.33g

Chocolate Chip Cookies

Preparation time: 10 minutes

Cook time: 10 minutes

Total time: 50 minutes

Servings: 12 Cookies

Ingredients:

- 6 ounces of Almond Flour (1 ½ cups)
- 3.5 ounces of Salted Butter (½ cup)
- ¾ cup of Erythritol (SoNourished) (4.5 ounces)
- 1 Teaspoon of Vanilla Extract
- 1 large Egg
- ½ Teaspoon of baking powder
- ¼ Teaspoon of Salt
- ½ Teaspoon of xanthan gum, optional
- 3 ounces of Sugar Free Chocolate Chips (30g - ¾ cup)

Cooking Instructions:

1. Preheat the oven to 180°C / 355°F. Add the butter in a microwave to melt. In a medium bowl, add the butter and beat with the erythritol.

2. Add together the vanilla and egg in a stand mixer. Blend on low speed for another 15 seconds. Add together the almond flour, xanthan gum, baking powder and salt.

3. Give everything a good mix until combined. Press the dough together and remove from the bowl. Add the chocolate chips into the dough and mix with your hands.

4. Roll the dough to make 12 balls. Transfer on a baking tray and bake for 10 minutes. Allow them to cool for a couple of minutes and serve.

5. Store in an airtight container for up to 7 days.

Nutrition Facts

Amount per Serving

Calories 168 Kcal | Fat 17.3g | Carbohydrates 2.3g | Protein 4g

Chewy Pecan Cookies

Yield: 20 cookies

Ingredients:

- 2 cups of ground pecans (250g)
- 1 large egg
- 1 tablespoon of salted butter, room temperature
- ½ teaspoon of baking soda
- ¼ cup of granulated sweetener (We used Sukrin Gold)
- 20 additional pecan halves to decorate, optional

Cooking Instructions:

1. Pre-heat the oven to 175°C /350°F. Use a food processor to grind the pecan halves. Add the remaining ingredients and give everything a good mix to combine.

2. Form the batter into little balls with your hand and flatten into a cookie. Line a baking tray with parchment paper and place the cookies.

3. If needed, add a pecan half on each cookie. Bake for 9-12 minutes or until the edges turns brown. Allow to cool for a couple of minutes to harden.

4. Serve and enjoy!

Nutrition Facts

Amounts per Serving

Calories: 101 Kcal | Fat: 11g | Carbohydrates: 1.9g | Protein: 1.6g

Pumpkin Cream Cheese Cookies

Servings: 16 Cookies

Ingredients:

- ½ cup of Coconut flour (56g)
- 3 ounces of Cream cheese softened (84g)
- ½ cup of Pumpkin puree (112g)
- ½ cup of Butter, unsalted softened (113g)
- ½ cup of Xylitol/Erythritol (107g)
- 1 Tsp. of Vanilla extract
- 1 ½ Tsp. of Pumpkin Spice
- ¼ Tsp. of Salt

Cooking Instructions:

1. Pre-heat the oven to 180°C/350°F. In a medium bowl, whisk together the butter and erythritol. Line a baking tray with parchment paper.

2. Add together the cream cheese, vanilla extra and pumpkin into the bowl. Whisk everything until smooth.

3. Add together the coconut flour, pumpkin spices and salt. Beat the ingredients until well combined. Use your hands to make the dough into balls.

4. Add the dough on a baking tray and repeat for the rest of the dough. Flatten the dough balls with spoon or spatula. Bake for 25 minutes until golden.

5. Allow to cool for a couple of minutes. Serve and enjoy!

Nutrition Facts

Amounts per Serving

Calories: 87 Kcal | Fat: 8g | Protein: 1g | Total Carbs: 3g |

Chocolate Chip Cookies

Preparation time: 5 minutes

Cook time: 15 minutes

Total time: 20 minutes

Ingredients:

- ¼ cup of coconut flour
- ⅓ cup of unsalted butter (room temperature)
- 3 tablespoons of Swerve sweetener
- 2 large eggs
- 3 tablespoons of sugar free chocolate chips
- ½ teaspoon of organic blackstrap molasses
- ¼ teaspoon of vanilla extract
- ⅛ teaspoon of salt

Cooking Instructions:

1. Preheat the oven to 350°F. In a medium bowl, add together the coconut flour, Swerve sweetener, chocolate chips, and salt and give everything a good mix.

2. In a large bowl, add together the unsalted butter, eggs, molasses, molasses, and vanilla extract and give everything a good mix.

3. Pour the wet ingredients into the dry ingredients. Add the cookies on a cookie mat, while measuring 2 tbsp. of batter.

4. Bake for 12-15 minutes until browned on the edges. Allow to cool for a couple of minutes.

5. Serve and enjoy!

Snickerdoodle Cookies

Preparation time: 10 minutes

Cook time: 12 minutes

Total time: 22 minutes

Yield: 16 large cookies

Ingredients:

For the Cookies:

- 2 eggs
- 2 teaspoons of vanilla extract
- 1 cup of almond butter
- ½ cup of almond milk
- ¼ cup of coconut oil, at room temperature
- 1 ½ cup of golden monk fruit sweetener
- 1 ¾ cup of almond flour
- 1 cup of coconut flour
- 1 teaspoon of baking soda
- 2 teaspoons of cream of tartar
- 1/8 teaspoon of pink Himalayan salt
- 1 teaspoon of cinnamon

For the Coating:

- 3 tablespoons of golden monk fruit sweetener
- 1 tablespoon of cinnamon

Cooking Instructions:

1. Preheat the oven to 350°F. Line the baking sheet with parchment paper.

2. In a large bowl, combine together the eggs, vanilla extract, almond butter, almond milk, and coconut oil with an electric mixer

3. In a different bowl, whisk together the dry ingredients. Pour the dry ingredients into the wet ingredients. Give everything a good mix to combine.

4. Refrigerate the batter bowl for about 15 minutes. Once chilled, form batter into medium-sized balls, fold the ball in cinnamon sugar coating mixture, and add on a baking sheet.

5. Flatten the balls with your hands into cookies. Bake for 10-12 minutes. Remove from oven and allow to cool for a couple of minutes. Serve and enjoy!

Chocolate Fudge Cookies

Preparation time: 10 minutes

Cook time: 15 minutes

Total time: 25 minutes

Servings: 10 Cookies

Ingredients:

- ½ cup of swerve confectioner
- ½ cup of Unsweetened Cocoa Powder
- ¼ cup of Butter
- 2 large Egg
- 1 teaspoon of vanilla extract
- 1 cup of Almond Flour
- 1 teaspoon of Baking powder
- 1 pinch of Pink Himalayan Salt

Cooking Instructions:

1. In a medium bowl, combine together the cocoa powder and swerve confectioners' sugar. Add the melted butter and combine the mixture with a hand mixer.

2. Add together the eggs, vanilla, and baking powder and mix again. Add the almond flour and mix again. Form the mixture into cookies.

3. Place the cookies on a greased baking sheet. Dust the tops of cookies with erythritol, if desired. Bake at 350°F for 12-15 minutes.

4. Allow to cool for a couple of minutes. Serve and enjoy!

Nutrition Facts

Amounts per Serving

Calories: 132kcal | Carbohydrates: 4.8g | Protein: 4.4g | Fat: 11.6g

Shortbread Cookies

Preparation time: 10 minutes

Cook time: 12 minutes

Total time: 22 minutes

Servings: 18

Ingredients:

- 2 ½ cups of Blanched almond flour
- 6 tablespoons of Butter
- ½ cup of Erythritol
- 1 teaspoon of Vanilla extract

Cooking Instructions:

1. Preheat the oven to 350°F / 177° C. Cover a cookie sheet with parchment paper. Beat together the butter and erythritol with hand mixer or stand mixer until fluffy.

2. Beat in the vanilla extract and almond flour. Pour rounded tablespoonful of the dough onto the cookie sheet. Flatten each cookie with a spoon or spatula.

3. Bake for about 12 minutes, or until the edges are golden. Allow to cool for a couple of minutes to harden.

Nutrition Facts

Amount per Serving

Calories: 124 Kcal | Fat 12g | Protein 3g | Total Carbs 3.3g

Flourless Chocolate Cookies

Preparation time: 10 minutes

Cook time: 12 minutes

Total time: 22 minutes

Servings: 24

Ingredients:

- 1 ½ cups of powdered Swerve sugar substitute
- 6 tbsp. of unsweetened cocoa powder
- ¼ tsp. of salt
- ½ cup of very dark chocolate chips 63%
- ½ cup of chopped pecans
- 3-4 large egg whites
- 1 tsp. of vanilla extract

Cooking Instructions:

1. Pre-heat the oven to 350°F. Line the baking sheet with parchment paper and spray with cooking spray.

2. In a medium bowl, mix together the Swerve, cocoa, salt, chocolate chips, and pecans. Add the vanilla with 3 egg whites and give everything a good stir.

3. Place rounded teaspoons of dough onto cookie sheet. Bake for 11-12 minutes. The cookies should be very soft in the center when removed from the oven.

4. Allow the cookies to cool for a couple of minutes. Place onto a cooling rack. Serve and enjoy!

Soft n' Chewy Cookies

Preparation time: 10 minutes

Cook time: 15 minutes

Total time: 25 minutes

Servings: 8

Ingredients:

- ¾ cup of almond meal
- ¼ cup of shredded coconut
- 1 tbsp. of baking powder
- ½ tsp. of stevia
- 1 tbsp. of coconut oil, melted
- 1 tsp. of vanilla extract
- 2 large eggs

Cooking Instructions:

1. In a medium bowl, combine together the almond meal, shredded coconut, stevia, and baking powder.

2. In a different bowl, combine together the wet ingredients. Pour the dry ingredients into the wet ingredients. Give everything a good mix to combine.

3. Place the dough on a cookie sheet, about 2" apart. It will make about 8 large cookies or 12 small cookies.

4. Bake the dough at 375°F for 15 minutes. Allow the cookies to cool for a couple of minutes. Transfer the cookies on a wire rack to cool completely.

5. Serve and enjoy!

Nutrition Facts

Amount per Serving

Calories: 107 Kcal | Total Fat: 8g 12% | Total Carbohydrates: 4g | Protein: 3g

Chocolate Butter Cookies

Preparation time: 10 minutes

Total time: 10 minutes

Yield: 10 Cookies

Ingredients:

- ¼ cup of creamy thick natural peanut butter
- ¼ cup of creamy thick natural almond butter
- 3 tbsp. of cream cheese, softened
- 2 tbsp. of salted butter, melted
- 1 tsp. of pure vanilla extract
- 2 tbsp. of unsweetened cocoa powder
- 2 tbsp. of confectioners erythritol
- ¾ cup of unsweetened desiccated coconut

Cooking Instructions:

1. Cover a baking sheet with a parchment paper. In a medium bowl, add together the peanut butter, almond butter, and cream cheese and give everything a good mix.

2. Add together the butter, vanilla extract, cocoa powder, and erythritol and give everything a good mix to combine.

3. Fold in the coconut with a rubber spatula. Give everything a good mix until the mixture is well combined.

4. Drop 1 ½ to 2 inch spoonful's onto the prepared baking sheet. Refrigerate for about for 10 minutes before serving. Store extras in the freezer.

5. Serve and enjoy!

BARS

Granola Bars

Preparation time: 15 minutes

Cook time: 20 minutes

Total time: 35 minutes

Servings: 16

Ingredients:

- ½ cup of drippy almond butter
- ¼ cup of coconut oil
- ¼ cup of golden monk fruit sweetener
- 1 egg white
- 1 tsp. of vanilla extract
- ½ tsp. of ground cinnamon
- ¼ tsp. of Himalayan sea salt
- 1 ½ cups of unsweetened flaked coconut
- 1 ¼ cups of sliced almonds
- 2/3 cup of chopped pecans
- ¼ cup of sunflower seeds
- 1 tbsp. of hemp seeds

Cooking Instructions:

1. Preheat the oven to 350°F. Cover an 8 x 8 baking dish with parchment paper. Set aside. In a large pot, add the almond butter, coconut oil, and monk fruit sweetener.

2. Cook the ingredients over medium heat, while stirring frequently until the monk fruit has dissolved. Remove pot from heat and allow mixture to cool for 3 minutes.

3. Whisk in cinnamon, salt, vanilla and egg white. Add in flaked coconut, sliced almonds, chopped pecans, sunflower seeds and hemp seeds.

4. Give everything a good stir to combine. Add the mixture into baking dish and flatten the surface with a spatula.

5. Bake in oven for 15-18 minutes, until edges are slightly brown. Remove pan from oven and allow to cool for couple of minutes.

6. Once cooled, take the parchment paper overhang to place the uncut bars onto a cutting board. Cut the edges of the bars into even rectangles with a sharp knife.

7. Store the bars in an airtight container or in the freezer for up to 3 months. Serve and enjoy!

Nutrition Facts

Amount per Serving

Calories: 223 Kcal | Total Fat: 21g | Total Carbohydrates: 6g | Protein 5g

Nut Bars

Preparation time: 10 minutes

Passive time: 1 hour

Servings: 10 bars

Ingredients:

- 2 cups of Mixed nuts and seeds, We used almonds, walnuts, pumpkin seeds and sunflower seeds, roughly chop the larger nuts
- ½ cup of desiccated coconut
- 1 tbsp. of chia seeds
- ¼ tsp. of salt
- 2 tbsp. of coconut oil or butter
- 1 tsp. of vanilla essence
- 3 tbsp. of almond butter or peanut butter
- 1/3 cup of Sukrin Gold Fiber Syrup See link

Cooking Instructions:

1. Cover a 20cm square baking tin with baking paper. In a medium bowl, combine together the desiccated coconut, chia seeds and salt.

2. In a small microwave proof bowl, add together the coconut oil/butter, vanilla, almond butter and fiber syrup. Microwave the oil and butter mixture for about 30 seconds to combine.

3. Give everything a good mix. Pour the melted mixture over the nuts and seeds and stir to combine. Press into the baking tin with the back of a measuring cup.

4. Refrigerate for 1 hour before cutting, or refrigerate until ready to eat. Store in the fridge or freezer. Serve when you are ready eat and enjoy.

Nutrition Facts

Amount per Serving

Calories: 268 Kcal | Total Fat: 22g | Total Carbohydrates: 15g | Protein 7g

Cookie Dough Bars

Preparation time: 10 minutes

Total time: 10 minutes

Servings: 8 Bars

Ingredients:

- ¾ cup of almond meal or almond flour
- 2 tbsp. of coconut flour
- ½ cup of peanut butter, unsalted, fresh, runny
- 2 tbsp. of sugar free maple flavored syrup -Monk Fruit
- 1/3 cup of sugar free chocolate chips
- Chocolate nut butter layer
- 3 ounces of sugar free dark chocolate
- 2 tbsp. of peanut butter, unsalted, fresh, runny

Cooking Instructions:

1. In a large bowl, add together the liquid sweetener and peanut butter. Microwave the mixture for 30 seconds and stir to combine. Set aside.

2. Add together the almond flour, coconut flour and chocolate chips. Give everything a good stir until fully incorporated. Place the dough into a rectangle loaf baking pan lined with a piece of parchment paper.

3. Press the dough with your hands and flatten the surface with a spatula. Freeze for a couple of minutes while you prepare the chocolate layer.

4. In a medium bowl, add together the sugar free dark chocolate and nut butter. Microwave for about 30 seconds to melt and stirring frequently.

5. Give everything a good stir to combine. Remove the loaf pan from the freezer, add the melted chocolate onto the bar and flatten the surface with a spatula.

6. Freeze again for about 12 minutes or until the chocolate layer is set. Use a sharp knife to cut the mixture into bars. Store in the fridge in a plastic bag for about 10 days!

Nutrition Facts

Amount per Serving

Calories: 198 Kcal | Carbohydrates: 9.9g | Protein 7.2g

Chocolate Crunch Bars

Preparation time: 5 minutes

Cook time: 5 minutes

Total time: 10 minutes

Servings: 20

Ingredients:

- 1 ½ cups of chocolate chips, We used stevia sweetened keto friendly chocolate chips
- 1 cup of almond butter, or substitute for any nut or seed butter of choice
- ½ cup of sticky sweetener
- ¼ cup of coconut oil
- 3 cups of nuts and seeds of choice almonds, cashews, pepitas etc

Cooking Instructions:

1. Cover an 8 x 8-inch baking dish with parchment paper. Set aside.

2. In a microwave-safe bowl, add together the chocolate chips of choice, almond butter, sticky sweetener and coconut oil.

3. Microwave the ingredients to melt and combine. Add your nuts/seeds of choice and give everything a good mix to combine.

4. Add the keto crunch bar mixture into the lined baking dish and flatten the surface with a spatula. Refrigerate or freeze until firm.

5. Serve and enjoy!

Nutrition Facts

Amounts per Serving

Calories: 155 Kcal | Carbohydrates: 4g | Protein: 7g | Fat: 12g

Protein Bars

Preparation time: 15 minutes

Cook time: 20 minutes

Total time: 35 minutes

Servings: 16 bars

Ingredients:

- ½ cup of drippy almond butter
- ¼ cup of coconut oil
- 1 egg white
- 1 tablespoon of vanilla extract
- ½ tablespoon of ground cinnamon
- ¼ tablespoon of Himalayan sea salt
- 1 scoop of your desired Protein powder (or swap with 1 tbsp. of almond flour)
- 1 ½ cup of unsweetened flaked coconut
- 1 ¼ cup of sliced almonds
- 2 2/3 cup of chopped pecans
- 1 ¼ cup of sunflower seeds
- ¼ cup of golden monk fruit sweetener

Cooking Instructions:

1. Preheat the oven to 350°F. Cover an 8 x 8 baking dish with parchment paper. Set aside.

2. In a large pot, add together the almond butter, coconut oil, monk fruit sweetener.

3. Cook the ingredients over medium heat, while stirring frequently until the monk fruit has melted. Remove pot from heat and cool the mixture for about 3 minutes.

4. Whisk in cinnamon, salt, vanilla and egg white. Add in protein powder, flaked coconut, sliced almonds, chopped pecans, sunflower seeds and hemp seeds and give everything a good stir until combined.

5. Place the mixture into prepared pan and flatten the surface with a spatula. Bake in the oven for 15-18 minutes, until the edges are slightly brown.

6. Remove the pan from oven and let to cool for a couple of minutes. Once cooled, transfer the uncut bars onto a cutting board with parchment paper overhang.

7. Cut the bars into even rectangles with a sharp knife. Store the bars in an airtight container in the freezer for up to 3 months.

8. Serve and enjoy!

Nutrition Facts

Amount per Serving

Calories: 313 Kcal | Total Fat: 32g | Total Carbohydrates: 8g | Protein 8g

Almond Joy Bars

Preparation time: 10 minutes

Cook time: 8 minutes

Total time: 18 minutes

Servings: 16 bars

Ingredients:

Chocolate / Carob Base

- ½ cup of organic coconut oil
- ½ cup of organic almond butter
- ¼ cup of xylitol (or your desired sweetener)
- 6 tablespoons of organic cocoa
- 4 tablespoons of organic erythritol
- 1 teaspoon of vanilla

Coconut Topping:

- 1 2/3 cup of organic unsweetened coconut flakes
- 7 tablespoons of coconut oil
- 1/3 cup of xylitol
- 1 ½ teaspoon of vanilla
- ¼ teaspoon of additional flavoring, optional
- 2 teaspoon of organic arrowroot powder
- Almond halves or slices, optional

Cooking Instructions:

Base:

1. Dissolve the oil and nut / seed butter over low heat. Stir in cocoa / carob and granulated sweetener and give everything a good stir to combine.

2. Stir in the rest of the ingredients except for vanilla. Continue to stir the mixture until it thickens slightly, then remove from heat. Stir in the vanilla.

3. Pour the mixture into an 8×8 pan. Add in the freezer to harden while you make the topping.

Topping:

4. Dissolve the oil in a small pan. Add the coconut flakes and stir well. Add rest of the ingredients and simmer, while stirring frequently until it thickens a bit.

5. Once the chocolate is hardened, carefully smooth the top with coconut mixture. Add slivered or whole almonds on top, if desired.

6. Place the bars in the freezer to harden. Slice the bars into squares of desired size and enjoy! Store in the refrigerator or freezer.

7. Serve and enjoy!

Chocolate Collagen Candy Bar

Servings: 2

Ingredients:

- 2 Bulletproof Vanilla Collagen Bars
- 2 tablespoons of Bulletproof Cacao Powder
- 2 medium chunks of Bulletproof Cacao Butter
- 2 tablespoons of Birch Xylitol, powdered
- 1 tablespoon of Brain Octane Oil
- 1 teaspoon of Vanillamax

Cooking Instructions:

1. Freeze the collagen bars to become stiff. Dissolve the cacao butter in a double-boiler. Powder the xylitol in a coffee grinder.

2. Add the remaining ingredients and give everything a good whisk until thick and creamy. Remove the bars from the freezer.

3. Unwrap the bars with a fork and dip one side of the bar into the chocolate. Arrange the bars bare side down on a glass dish covered with parchment paper.

4. Repeat the procedure with the remaining bars. Place in freezer until solid. Remove the bars from the freezer.

5. Repeat the procedure with the bare side of the bar and place back in freezer. Do as many coatings as you like to get your desired finishing coat.

6. Serve and enjoy!

Lemon Bars

Preparation time: 10 minutes

Cook time: 28 minutes

Total time: 38 minutes

Servings: 16

Ingredients:

Shortbread crust:

- 2 ½ cups of Blanched almond flour
- 1/3 cup of LC Foods erythritol
- ¼ teaspoon of sea salt
- ¼ cup of coconut oil, melted
- 1 large egg, whisked
- ½ teaspoon of vanilla extract

Lemon filling:

- ½ cup of LC Foods powdered erythritol
- ¼ cup of Blanched almond flour
- 4 large eggs
- ¾ cup of lemon juice
- 1 tablespoon of lemon zest

Cooking Instructions:

1. Preheat the oven to 350°F / 177°C. Cover 9x9 inch (23x23 cm) pan with parchment paper. In a medium bowl, stir together the almond flour and powdered sweetener.

2. Whisk in the eggs, lemon juice, and lemon zest, until smooth. Set aside. In a different bowl, combine together the almond flour, erythritol and sea salt.

3. Stir in the melted coconut oil, then the egg and vanilla. Press the dough into the lined pan and flatten the surface with a spatula.

4. Bake for about 13 to 16 minutes, until golden. Remove the crust from heat and pour the filling over the crust. Place back in the oven for 15 minutes, until filling is set.

5. Allow to cool for a couple of minutes. Cover and refrigerate for at least 2 hours before slicing. Serve and enjoy!

Nutrition Facts

Calories: 166 Kcal | Fat: 14g | Protein: 6g | Total Carbs: 5g

Snickers Bars

Servings: 6

Preparation time: 20 minutes

Total time: 50 minutes

Ingredients:

"Crème" Layer:

- ⅓ cup of cashews, soaked, unsalted
- 1 ½ tablespoon of coconut cream
- 1 ½ tablespoon of brown erythritol (or 1 tablespoon/15g) Golden Monk Fruit Sweetener)
- ½ teaspoon of sugar-free vanilla extract, optional

"Caramel" Layer:

- 3 tablespoons of all natural peanut butter (no sugar added)
- 2 teaspoons of sticky sweetener (like this sugar-free maple syrup))
- 1 tablespoon of granulated erythritol
- 2 tablespoons of melted butter
- A handful of whole peanuts

Chocolate Layer:

- 50g of sugar-free chocolate or chocolate with at least 85% cacoa content
- 2.6 ounces / 75g of additional chocolate for top coat, optional

Cooking Instructions:

1. Add together all the crème layer ingredients like soaked cashews, coconut cream, brown erythritol & vanilla extract into a food processor.

2. Blend all the ingredients for about 1-2 minutes or until smooth. Refrigerate for a couple of minutes. Dissolve the sugar-free chocolate with a double boiler.

3. Add the chocolate into rectangular shaped silicone molds. Transfer the mold with the chocolate in your freezer for about 10 minutes or until the chocolate has hardened.

4. Add the cashew crème into the silicone mold. Make the crème to form shapes with your fingers. Place back in your freezer for about 15 minutes.

5. In a large bowl, mix together all of the caramel layer ingredients except for the whole peanuts. Add the caramel layer on top of the crème layer into the silicone mold.

6. Add the whole peanuts on top of the caramel layer and refrigerate again for about 15 minutes. Dissolve the additional chocolate and pour over the finished "naked" bars.

7. Serve the snicker bars with a hot cup of tea or coffee! Store in your fridge for up to 1 week. Serve and enjoy!

Nutrition Facts

Amount per Serving

Calories: 214 Kcal | Total Fat: 18.9g | Carbohydrate: 6.3g | Protein: 5g

Peanut Butter Chocolate Bars

Preparation time: 10 minutes

Total time: 10 minutes

Servings: 8

Ingredients:

For the Bars:

- ¾ cup of Almond Flour
- 2 ounces of Butter
- ¼ cup of Swerve Icing sugar style
- ½ cup of Creamy Peanut Butter
- Vanilla extract

For the Topping:

- ½ cup of Sugar-Free Chocolate Chips

Cooking Instructions:

1. In a 6 inch pan, mix together all of the bar ingredients. Dissolve the chocolate chips in a microwave oven for 30 seconds and give everything a good stir.

2. Add additional 10 seconds, if desired to completely melt. Spread the topping on top of the bars. Refrigerate for about 1 or 2 hours to harden the bars.

3. Serve and enjoy!

Nutrition Facts

Amounts per Serving

246 Kcal | Fat: 23g | Carbohydrates: 7g | Protein: 7g

Magic Bars

Total time: 45 minutes

Yield: 12-16 bars

Ingredients:

- 1 ½ cups of almond flour (nut-free version)
- 2 tablespoons of sweetener of choice, or stevia
- 3 tablespoons of melted coconut oil
- ¼ teaspoon of salt
- ¾ cup of mini chocolate chips or sugar free chocolate chips
- ¼ cup of finely chopped walnuts, optional
- 2/3 cup of full-fat shredded coconut
- 1 ¼ cup of full-fat canned coconut milk
- 2 tablespoons of cocoa powder, optional

Cooking Instructions:

1. Pre-heat the oven to 350°F. Cover an 8-inch pan with parchment paper. In a medium bowl, combine together the almond flour, oil, salt, and sweetener.

2. Press the dough into the pan. Sprinkle the chocolate chips, coconut, and optional nuts over top. Mix the coconut milk and cocoa and pour the mixture over the top.

3. Bake for 33 minutes. Remove from the oven and allow to cool for about 15 minutes. Slice into bars and enjoy!

Nutrition Facts

Amounts per Serving

Calories: 132 Kcal | Total Fat: 12.4g | Total Carbohydrate: 6.9g | Protein: 1.8g

Fathead Blueberry Bars

Yield: 12 squares

Preparation time: 30 minutes

Cook time: 30 minutes

Total time: 1 hour

Calories: 159 Kcal

Ingredients:

- ½ stick butter, softened
- 1 egg, beaten
- ½ cup of sweetener
- 1 ¼ cup of almond flour
- 1 teaspoon of vanilla
- 1 teaspoon of cinnamon
- 2 tablespoons of sour cream
- Zest of lemon
- 2 oz. of cream cheese
- 1 ½ cup of mozzarella
- 2 cups of blueberries
- 2 teaspoons of xantham gum

Cooking Instructions:

1. Dissolve the mozzarella and cream cheese in a microwave safe dish. Give everything a good stir until smooth.

2. In a different bowl, cream together the butter, egg, almond flour, vanilla, sweetener, cinnamon and sour cream. Pour the cheese mixture into batter and stir to combine into a soft dough.

3. Add more almond flour if dough is too sticky. Pour the mixture onto parchment paper or plastic wrap and roll them into ball.

4. Wrap the ball and refrigerate while preparing blueberries. In a sauce pan over medium low heat, add the blueberries and cook, while mixing often.

5. Once enough juice has formed, bring to a boil. Stir in xantham gum. When the sauce thickens, reduce to simmer.

6. Add the lemon zest and give everything a good stir. Remove from heat and set aside. Preheat the oven to 400°F. Pour ¾ of the dough into greased 9x9 pan.

7. Bake the dough for about 10 minutes. Remove from the oven and allow to cool for about 5 minutes. Pour the blueberry mixture into crust.

8. Spread the mixture evenly. Top with rest of the dough. Bake in the oven for about 10-15 more minutes or until golden brown and set.

9. Allow to cool for a couple of minutes. Slice and serve.

Cookie Bars

Preparation time: 10 minutes

Cook time: 15 minutes

Total time: 25 minutes

Serves: 16

- **Ingredients:**
- ¾ cup of coconut butter
- ¼ cup of unsweetened apple sauce
- ¼ tsp. of grey sea salt
- 1 ¼ cup of raw sesame seeds

Optional:

- ½ tsp. of ground cinnamon
- ½ tsp. of vanilla extract
- 5-10 drops alcohol-free stevia

Cooking Instructions:

1. Preheat the oven to 350°F. Prepare a 16-count silicon baking mold sheet or small muffin silicon molds and set aside.

2. In a medium bowl, add together the coconut butter, applesauce and sea salt. Add the optional ingredients, if desired.

3. Give everything a good stir to combine. Add in sesame seeds and stir to coat. Press the dough into prepared sheet.

4. Bake in the oven for 10-15 minutes, until top turns brown. Remove from the oven, and allow to cool for about 20 minutes.

5. Transfer the bars to the freezer to chill for additional 20 minutes to firm up. Store at room temperature. Serve and enjoy!

Chocolate Fudge Protein Bars

Preparation time: 10 minutes

Total time: 10 minutes

Servings: 16

Ingredients:

- 4 oz. of raw unsalted sunflower seeds
- 4 oz. of sun butter or tahini
- 2.7 oz. of chocolate protein powder(We used Quest)
- 3 oz. of unsweetened cocoa powder
- ¾ cup of Sukrin Melis (powdered sugar free sweetener)
- ½ teaspoon of salt
- 8 tablespoons of softened coconut oil
- ½ cup of sugar free chocolate chips and 1 tablespoon of butter, optional for coating

Cooking Instructions:

1. Line a loaf pan with parchment paper. Add together all of the ingredients into a food processor. Blend everything until smooth. Scrape down sides and blend again.

2. Taste and adjust the sweetener to suit your desired taste. Pour batter into a prepared loaf pan. Refrigerate for 30 minutes.

3. Slice into 8 bars with a knife, then cut bars in half to make 16 bars. Freeze for about 30 minutes if you desired making the optional coating.

4. Melt the chocolate chips and butter in microwave for 1 minute, if your desire the optional coating. Give everything a good stir until smooth.

5. Dredge the bottom half of the bars into the melted chocolate and transfer on a parchment lined baking sheet. Drizzle more chocolate on top of bars if desired.

6. Serve and enjoy!

Nutrition Facts

Amount per Serving

Calories: 159 Kcal | Total Fat: 14.8g | Total Carbohydrates: 3.6g | Protein: 6.7g

TARTS

Chocolate & Lime Tarts

Hands-on: 15 minutes

Overall time: 1 hour

Yield: 6-12 tarts

Ingredients:

Base:

- 1 ¼ cups of almond flour
- 3 tablespoons of whey protein powder or egg white protein powder
- 1 medium egg
- 1 ½ tablespoon of coconut oil
- 2 ½ tablespoons of Erythritol or Swerve, optional

Filling:

- 3 large ripe avocados (600g)
- 2 tablespoons of Erythritol, Swerve or other keto-friendly sweetener to taste
- 2 tablespoons of virgin coconut oil, soft but not melted
- Juice of 1 ½ limes
- 1/3 cup of raw cacao
- 1/8 teaspoon of sea salt

Decoration:

- 2-3 squares dark 99% chocolate (unsweetened chocolate), shaved OR 85-90% dark chocolate
- Zest from ½ lime

Cooking Instructions:

1. Make the low carb tart bases. Bake the crust until golden, remove from the oven and allow to cool for a couple of minutes.

2. Make the filling by removing the skins and stones from the avocados. In a medium bowl, add together the avocado meat, sweetener. Taste and adjust to taste.

3. Add the coconut oil, lime juice, salt and cacao. Blend the ingredients with a hand blender until smooth. Taste and adjust the sweetness to taste.

4. Divide the chocolate filling into 6. Fill each of the keto tart crusts and flatten the top with a spatula. Refrigerate for at least an hour or until set.

5. Grate the dark chocolate and lime zest. Take out keto chocolate tarts from the fridge and top with grated chocolate and lime zest.

6. Place in the fridge until ready to serve. Serve with keto vanilla soft scoop ice cream, full-fat plain Greek yogurt or coconut yogurt.

Nutritional Facts

Amounts per Serving

Calories: 400 Kcal | Carbohydrate: 6.1g | Protein: 11.1g | Fat: 36.1g

Bakewell Tarts

Preparation time: 5 minutes

Cook time: 15 mins

Total time: 20 mins

Servings: 6 mini cupcakes

Ingredients:

- 220 g butter softened
- 8 tablespoons of granulated sweetener
- 200 g of almond meal/flour
- 2 eggs medium
- 1-2 teaspoon of almond extract
- Sliced almonds for decoration

Cooking Instructions:

1. In a medium bowl, combine together the softened butter and sweetener. Add together the almond flour/meal and give everything a good mix.

2. Add the egg and almond extract and give everything a good mix until smooth. Divide the mixture evenly between 12 mini cupcake cases.

3. Press a few almond slices into the top of each cupcake. Bake at 180°C/350°F for 15 minutes, or until golden brown.

4. Allow to cool for a couple of minutes. Once cooled, sprinkle with some powdered sweetener. Serve and enjoy!

Nutrition Facts

Amount per Serving

Calories: 237 Kcal | Total Fat: 23g | Total Carbohydrates: 3g | Protein: 4g

Strawberry Tart

Preparation time: 10 minutes

Total time: 10 minutes

Servings: 8

Ingredients:

Crust:

- 1.5 cups of almond flour
- 3 tablespoons of butter, cut into pieces
- ¼ cup of Trim Healthy Mama Gentle Sweet or any sweetener

Filling:

- 16 ounces of cream cheese
- ½ cup of Trim Healthy Mama Gentle Sweet or my sweetener, ground
- 2-4 cups of strawberries, quartered

Cooking Instructions:

1. In a food processor, combine together the crust ingredients and blend until smooth. Pour the dough into the bottom of a 9-inch tart pan.

2. Add together the cream cheese and sweetener to the food processor. Blend the ingredients until smooth. Spread the blended mixture on top of the crust.

3. Top with the strawberries. Refrigerate for at least 2-3 hours before serving. Serve and enjoy!

Nutrition Facts

Amount per Serving

Calories: 362 Kcal | Total Fat: 34g | Total Carbohydrates: 9g | Protein 8g

Chocolate Espresso Mini Tarts

Hands-on: 15 minutes

Overall time: 1 hour 15 minutes

Yield: 4 mini tarts

Ingredients:

Crust:

- ¾ cup of almond flour
- 2 tablespoons of dark cocoa powder
- 2 tablespoons of virgin coconut oil
- 1 tablespoon of granulated Erythritol or Swerve
- 1 teaspoon of sugar-free vanilla extract
- Dash of sea salt

Filling:

- ½ cup of melted virgin coconut oil
- 1/3 cup of coconut cream
- 2 tablespoons of cocoa powder or Dutch process cocoa powder
- 1/3 cup of unsweetened chocolate chunks, melted
- ¼ cup of powdered Erythritol or Swerve
- 1 tablespoon of instant coffee powder
- ¼ teaspoon of sugar-free vanilla extract
- Dash of sea salt

Cooking Instructions:

1. Combine together all of the crust ingredients until a crumbly dough forms. Divide the dough into half and pour into two 10 cm/ 4" mini tart pans.

2. For the filling, simmer the coconut cream and add in the espresso powder. Give everything a good stir until the powder has melted.

3. Place the mixture into a bowl. Add the rest of the ingredients to the bowl and give everything a good mix until smooth. Divide the mixture between the two tart pans.

4. Place to the refrigerator and refrigerate for at least 1 hour before serving. Top with some coffee beans, if desired. Store refrigerated for up to 5 days.

Nutritional Facts

Calories: 296 Kcal | Carbohydrate: 3.2g | Protein: 4g | Fat: 29.4g

Dough Tart

Yields: 6

Preparation time: 10 minutes

Cook time: 1 minutes

Total time: 11 minutes

Ingredients:

- Almond Flour
- 1 cup of Almond Flour
- ⅛ tsp. of salt
- ¼ tsp. of Baking Powder
- 3 tbsp. of Butter, Salted
- 1 large Raw Egg Yolk
- ⅛ cup of Almond Milk

Cooking Instructions:

1. Combine together the almond flour, salt and baking powder in a stand mixer with a paddle attachment. Cut the butter into about 12 cubes.

2. Mix them into the four. Mix everything until you have chunks that are 1-2 inches long. Then, mix in the egg yolk.

3. Mixing 1 tablespoon at a time, mix in the almond milk or until the dough is formed. Press the dough into a flat disc and wrap it in plastic wrap.

4. Refrigerate the tart dough to cool. Store in the fridge for at least 1 week. To defrost tart dough, allow it to thaw in a refrigerator.

5. Serve and enjoy!

Nutrition Facts

Amounts per Serving

Calories: 167 Kcal | Total Carbs: 3.8g | Protein: 4.4g | Fat: 15.9g

Chocolate Hazelnut Tart

Preparation time: 10 minutes

Cook time: 0 minutes

Yield: 8

Ingredients:

- 4 Keto mini pie crusts
- 2 tbsp. of coconut oil, melted
- 2 tbsp. of coconut cream, melted
- 2 ounces of 100% chocolate, melted
- Erythritol, to taste
- ¼ cup of hazelnut butter

Cooking Instructions:

1. In a medium bowl, combine together the coconut oil, coconut cream, chocolate, and erythritol. Add 1 tbsp. of hazelnut butter in each tart crust.

2. Pour the chocolate mixture on top of the hazelnut butter filling. Refrigerate for 2 at least 4 hours or until set.

3. Serve and enjoy!

Nutrition Facts

Amounts per Serving

Calories: 223 Kcal | Fat: 18g | Carbohydrates: 7g | Protein: 6 g

Butter Tarts

Preparation time: 30 minutes

Cook time: 20 minutes

Total time: 50 minutes

Yield: 8

Ingredients:

Crust:

- ¾ cup of coconut flour
- ½ cup of butter, melted
- 2 eggs
- 3 tablespoons of sugar substitute (We used xylitol)

Filling:

- 2 eggs
- 1/3 cup of softened butter
- 1 cup of packed Sukrin Gold (or another brown sugar)
- 1 teaspoon of vanilla
- 4 tablespoons of heavy cream

Cooking Instructions:

1. Combine together the coconut flour, eggs, sugar substitute and melted butter in a mixing bowl. Give everything a good stir to combine.

2. Scoop some of the crust into greased muffin tins. Cover the bottom and sides of the tins. Press down and allow a small 'pool' area for the filling. Set aside.

3. In a small pot, add together filling ingredients and whisk. Heat the filling on medium heat, stirring constantly.

4. Whisk the filling until the butter has dissolve and is incorporated into your filling. Remove the filling from heat and allow to rest for about 2-3 minutes.

5. Take a ladle, large spoon and pour the filling into the shells. Bake at 350°F / 175°C for 15-20 minutes or until the top turn's golden.

6. Allow to cool for about 5-10 minutes. Serve and enjoy!

Nutrition Facts

Calories: 210 Kcal | Total Fat: 18.3g | Carbohydrates: 6.4g | Protein: 4.9g

Tart Crust

Preparation time: 10 minutes

Cook time: 15 minutes

Total time: 25 minutes

Servings: 12

Ingredients:

- 1 - ½ cups of almond flour
- ½ cup of coconut flour
- 5 tablespoons of Eryrthritol, powdered
- 2 large eggs
- 4 tablespoons of unsalted butter, cold
- ½ teaspoon of vanilla extract

Cooking Instructions:

1. Preheat the oven to 350°F. Spray a 10 inch tart pan with cooking spray. Set aside. In a food processor, add together all of the ingredients.

2. Blend the ingredients until well combined. Press the dough with a spoon into the bottom of the greased tart pan.

3. Bake in the oven at 350°F for about 15 minutes or until top turns brown. Remove the crust from the oven and allow to cool for about 10 minutes.

4. Remove tart from pan and fill as needed. Serve and enjoy!

Nutrition Facts

Amounts per Serving

Calories: 146 Kcal | Carbohydrates: 6.1g | Protein: 5.1g | Fat: 12g

Cheesecake Tarts

Ingredients:

The Dough:

- ½ Cup of Almond Flour
- ½ Cup of Coconut Flour
- 2 Tablespoons of Psyllium Husk Powder
- 2 Tablespoons of Coconut Oil
- 2 Large Eggs
- 5 Tablespoons of Ice Cold Water
- ½ Teaspoon of Pure Vanilla Extract
- ¼ Teaspoon of Liquid Stevia

The Cheesecake:

- 5 Ounces of Cream Cheese
- 1 Large Egg
- ¼ Cup of Erythritol, powdered
- ⅓ Cup of Sour Cream
- ½ Teaspoon of Pure Vanilla Extract
- 10 drops of Liquid Stevia

The Compote:

- 3 Ounces of Blackberries
- Juice & Zest from ½ Lemon
- 2 Tablespoons of Erythritol, powdered

Cooking Instructions:

1. In a medium bowl, mix together all of the dry ingredients for the tart dough. In a separate bowl, mix together the wet ingredients.

2. Pour the dry ingredients into the wet ingredients. Press the dough together and form a block. Cut the block into 4 and line the inside of a tart pan.

3. Pre-heat the oven to 350°F. Bake the dough for 12-15 minutes. Powder the erythritol in a spice grinder and mix all of the cheesecake ingredients with a hand mixer.

4. Add erythritol to the cheesecake mix and give everything a good mix. When done, fill tart pans and bake in the oven for about 25-30 minutes.

5. Meanwhile, add blackberries to pan over medium-low heat. Once the blueberries starts to release their juice, lightly crush them and add the remaining ingredients.

6. Simmer to reduce the sauce to your liking. Top the cheesecakes with the blackberry compote and add a dollop of whipped cream.

7. Serve and enjoy!

Toasted Cream Tarts

Hands-on: 15 minutes

Overall time: 3 hours

Yield: 24 tarts

Ingredients:

Toasted Cream:

- 500 ml cream
- ¼ teaspoon of baking soda
- 1 tablespoon of Sukrin Gold, Swerve or Erythritol (10 g)
- ¼ teaspoon of cinnamon

Tart Shells:

- 1 ½ cups of shredded low-moisture mozzarella cheese
- 1 heaped tablespoon of cream cheese
- ¾ cup + 1 tablespoon of almond flour
- 1 large egg
- 1 tablespoon of Sukrin Gold, Swerve or other brown sugar substitute
- ¼ teaspoon of cinnamon
- Olive oil or coconut oil

Cooking Instructions:

1. Make the toasted cream in an Instant Pot or pressure cooker. Pour the cream into a jug and add the bicarb soda and give everything a good mix.

2. Pour the mixture into jars. Transfer the jars to the steam rack of your pressure cooker. Pour about 2.5 cm/ 1 inch of cold water into the bottom of the pot.

3. Place the steam rack and stand the jars of cream on the rack. Close and lock the lid in place. Select Manual, High Pressure for 2 hours.

4. When the timer beeps, allow cream to cool inside the pressure cooker. Remove from pressure cooker. Place jars in fridge until chilled.

5. Preheat the oven to 220 °C/ 430 °F. In a microwave safe bowl, add together the mozzarella and cream cheese. Microwave on high for 1 minute.

6. Give everything a good stir. Microwave on high for additional 30 seconds. Add together the almond flour, egg, sweetener and cinnamon and give everything a good stir to combine.

7. Roll out between two sheets of silicone paper. Cut out circles slightly larger than mini-muffin holes with a cookie cutter. Repeat the process to the remaining dough.

8. Spray your muffin tray with olive oil or grease with coconut oil. Carefully press the dough into the muffin holes and flatten the top with your fingers.

9. Bake in the oven for 15 minutes. Remove from oven and allow to cool for a couple of minutes. Whip cream with 1 tbsp. of Sukrin Gold and pipe into tart shells.

10. Dust the tart with the remaining cinnamon. Store in a container in the refrigerator for up to 4 days. Serve and enjoy!

Nutritional Facts

Amounts per Serving

Calories: 124 Kcal | Carbohydrate: 1.3g | Protein: 3.1g | Fat: 11.7g

PIES

Sweet Pie Crust

Hands-on 10 minutes

Overall: 25 minutes

Yield: 8

Ingredients:

- 1 ¾ cup of almond flour
- ¼ cup of vanilla or plain whey protein or egg white protein powder
- ¼ cup of Erythritol or Swerve, powdered
- 1 large egg
- 2 tablespoons of extra virgin coconut oil or ghee
- **Optionally Add In:**
- 1 teaspoon of vanilla extract
- ½ - 1 teaspoon of cinnamon
- 1 teaspoon of pumpkin spice mix or
- 1 teaspoon of food extract of your choice (chocolate, almond, lemon, etc.)

Cooking Instructions:

1. Preheat the oven to 175 °C/ 350 °F. In a medium bowl, combine together the almond flour, whey protein and powdered Erythritol.

2. Add the egg and coconut oil. Give everything a good stir to combine. Add the dough into a non-stick pan with a removable bottom.

3. Press up the sides with a dough roller to form a "bowl" shape. Line the bottom of the pan with baking sheet. Place in the oven. Bake for 12-15 minutes.

4. Once done, remove from the heat and fill with your desired filling like keto lemon curd, whipped cream, creamed coconut milk, low-carb custard, and chocolate.

5. Allow the pie crust to cool for a couple of minutes. Store in an airtight container and keep at room temperature. Serve and enjoy!

Nutritional Facts

Amounts per Serving

Calories: 181 Kcal | Carbohydrate: 2.3 g | Protein: 8.4 g | Fat: 15.5 g

Lemon Meringue Pie

Ingredients:

Crust:

- 2 eggs
- 2 tbsp. of Swerve granulated sweetener
- 1 tsp. of vanilla extract
- ½ cup of butter, cut in small cubes
- 2 tsp. of arrowroot
- ½ cup of almond flour
- ½ cup of coconut flour

Filling:

- 1 ¼ cups of Swerve granulated sugar
- 1 envelope of unflavored gelatin
- ¼ tsp. of salt
- 1 tbsp. of arrowroot
- 1 ¼ cup of water
- 4 large egg yolks, beaten
- ½ cup of fresh squeezed lemon juice
- 3 tbsp. of butter
- 2 tsp. of grated lemon zest

Meringue:

- 4 egg whites
- ½ tsp. of cream of tartar
- ½ cup of Swerve granulated sugar

Cooking Instructions:

1. Preheat the oven to 350°F. In a food processor, add together all the crust ingredients and pulse until it is crumbly. Mold the mixture into pie pan.

2. Bake for 10 – 12 minutes. In a sauce pan, combine together the sugar, gelatin, salt and water and bring to a boil stirring constantly.

3. Simmer for 1 minute and pour some into beaten eggs. Pour egg mixture into the saucepan and simmer until thickened.

4. Whisk in lemon juice, butter and lemon zest. Remove the saucepan from heat and set aside. In a medium bowl, beat the egg whites and cream of tartar.

5. Blend on low speed until it becomes foamy. Gently add sugar and keep on beating until stiff peaks form. Pour hot filling into pie crust and top with meringue.

6. Seal the edges and mound extra meringue in the middle. Bake for 30 minutes or until lightly browned.

7. Allow to cool for about 1 hour. Refrigerate for at least 3 hours to set up. Serve and enjoy!

Samoa Pie

Preparation time: 15 minutes

Total time: 15 minutes

Servings: 12

Ingredients:

No Bake Chocolate Crust:

- ½ cup of sunflower seeds raw, unsalted
- ½ cup of unsweetened cocoa powder
- ½ cup of coconut flour
- ½ cup of Swerve Confectioners sweetener
- ½ teaspoon of salt
- 8 tablespoons of butter soft

Filling:

- 16 oz. of heavy whipping cream
- 1 teaspoon of vanilla liquid stevia
- 8 oz. of cream cheese softened

Topping:

- ½ cup of Coconut flakes unsweetened, toasted
- 2 oz. of Microwave Salted Caramel Sauce or Choczero Caramel sauce
- 2 oz. of Sugar-Free Chocolate Chips, We used Lily's Sweets
- 3 teaspoons of butter

Cooking Instructions:

1. In a food processor, add together all the pie crust ingredients, and blend until smooth. Press into a 9 inch pie plate. Set aside.

2. Add the heavy cream and vanilla stevia into a stand mixer on high until whipped. Taste and adjust sweetener if desired and set aside.

3. Add the cream cheese in the mixer using the paddle blade attachment. Blend the cream cheese on high until smooth.

4. Roll the whipped cream with your hands and place into the stand mixer to combine with the cream cheese. Blend until smooth, spread into the pie crust.

5. In a medium bowl, stir together the coconut flakes and caramel sauce. Spread the mixture evenly over the pie.

6. Place the chocolate chips and butter in a microwave for 30 second intervals until melted. Give everything a good stir.

7. Drizzle over the coconut flake topping. Refrigerate for at least 2-3 hours or overnight. Serve and enjoy!

Nutrition Facts

Amount per Serving

Calories: 391 Kcal | Fat: 37g | Total Carbohydrates: 9g | Protein: 4g

Mini Chicken Pot Pies

Hands-on: 35 minutes

Overall: 1 hour

Yield: 4 medium pies

Ingredients:

Crust:

- ½ cup of butter, melted
- 2 large eggs
- ¾ cup + 1 tbsp. of coconut flour
- 1 tablespoon of psyllium husk, optional
- ¼ teaspoon of sea salt
- 1 large egg + 1 tablespoon of water

Filling:

- ¼ cup of unsalted butter
- ½ large white onion, diced
- 3 cloves garlic, minced
- 1 teaspoon of minced fresh herbs (sage, rosemary, thyme)
- 1 (10-ounces) bag frozen peas/carrots, thawed
- ½ cup of frozen green beans, thawed
- 1 pound of cooked chicken, shredded
- ½ cup of chicken broth
- 1 ½ cups of heavy cream
- Salt and pepper, to taste

Cooking Instructions:

1. Preheat the oven to 190°C/375°F. Add 4 medium ramekins on a baking sheet. In a medium bowl, combine together the eggs, coconut flour, and salt.

2. Add the psyllium husk if desired. Give everything a good mix until crumbly, then pour in the butter. Form into a ball and chill until ready to bake.

3. Melt the butter in a large skillet over medium heat. Add in the onion, garlic, and herbs. Cook the ingredients for about 3-4 minutes or until soft.

4. Add in the thawed vegetables, shredded chicken, and broth. Cook for about 3 minutes or until broth has mostly absorbed.

5. Pour in the heavy cream and bring to a boil until thick for about 5-7 minutes. Taste and adjust with salt and pepper to taste. Pour the filling into the ramekins.

6. Roll out the dough between two pieces of parchment 1/4-inch (1/2 cm) thick. Cut the dough with a sharp knife slightly larger than the ramekin.

7. Slowly flip onto the filled ramekins using the parchment. Pinch the sides together and fix any cracks. Repeat the same process until all ramekins are covered.

8. Whisk together an egg and 1 tbsp. of water. Brush over the crusts. Place in the oven. Bake for 20 minutes or until golden brown. Serve and enjoy!

Nutrition Facts

Amounts per Serving

Calories: 560 Kcal | Carbs: 7.3 g | Protein: 24.7 g | Fat: 45.3 g

Greek Spinach Pie

Preparation time: 15 minutes

Cook time: 35 minutes

Total time: 50 minutes

Servings: 18 slices

Ingredients:

Crust:

- 2 ½ cup of Blanched almond flour
- ½ teaspoon of Sea salt
- ¼ cup of Coconut oil (solid, then melted)
- 1 large Egg, beaten

Filling:

- 1 pound of Frozen spinach, defrosted and squeezed
- 8 ounces of Feta cheese, crumbled
- 4 ounces of Cream cheese, cut into small cubes
- 2 ounces of Mozzarella cheese (shredded)
- 4 cloves Garlic, minced
- 1 tablespoon of Fresh dill, chopped
- 4 large Egg, beaten

Cooking Instructions:

1. Preheat the oven to 350°F / 177°C. Cover the bottom of a 9 inch round pie pan with parchment paper. In a mixing bowl, combine the almond flour and sea salt.

2. Add in the melted coconut oil and egg and give everything a good stir until well combined. Press the dough into the bottom of the prepared pan.

3. Bake for about 10-12 minutes, or until golden. Stir in all the filling ingredients. Add the filling into it and flatten the top with spatula.

4. Bake for about 30-40 minutes, until the middle is firm. Allow to cool for a couple of minutes. Serve and enjoy!

Nutrition Facts

Amount per Serving

Calories: 238 Kcal | Fat: 20g | Protein: 10g | Total Carbs: 6g

Lemon Coconut Custard Pie

Preparation time: 10 minutes

Cook time: 45 minutes

Total time: 55 minutes

Servings: 8

Ingredients:

- 2 large eggs
- 1 cup of coconut milk canned
- ¾ cup of low carb sweetener
- ¼ cup of coconut flour
- 2 tbsp. of unsalted butter, melted
- 1 tsp. of vanilla extract
- ¾ tsp. of baking powder
- 1 tsp. of lemon zest
- ½ tsp. of lemon extract
- 4 Oz. of Unsweetened Shredded Coconut

Cooking Instructions:

1. Grease a 9-inch pie dish with cooking spray. Pre-heat the oven to 350°F. In a medium bowl, add together the eggs, coconut milk, sweetener, and coconut flour.

2. Add the butter, baking powder, vanilla, lemon zest, and lemon extract and give everything a good stir to combine. Fold in the unsweetened coconut.

3. Add the mixture into the prepared pie dish. Bake in the oven for about 40-45 minutes or until golden. Remove from the oven and allow to cool.

4. Once cooled, cut the pie with a sharp knife. Store leftovers in the refrigerator for up to 3 days. Serve and enjoy!

Nutrition Facts

Amount per Serving

Calories: 209 Kcal | Total Fat: 19g | Total Carbohydrates: 6g | Protein: 3g

Chocolate Almond Butter Pie

Yield: 12 slices of pie

Ingredients:

Crust:

- ¾ cup of coconut flour
- 2 tablespoons of psyllium husk
- ½ cup of coconut oil
- ½ cup of water
- Pinch salt

Filling:

- 2 ounces of unsweetened chocolate (We used Ghiradelli 100%)
- 1 can of full fat coconut milk
- ¼ cup of coconut oil
- 1 cup of almond butter
- ¼ teaspoon of stevia, optional

Cooking Instructions:

1. Preheat the oven to 350°F. In a medium bowl, add together the water and coconut oil to melt. Stir in psyllium husk until a sort of gel forms.

2. Stir in coconut flour and salt and allow it to rest for about 1-2 minutes or until all the liquid has been absorbed. Press the crust into a 9" pie dish.

3. Poke the bottom of the crust a bunch of times with a fork and place in the oven. Bake for 30 minutes.

4. In a high speed blender, combine the rest of the ingredients and blend until they are combined. Remove the crust from the oven.

5. Allow the crust to cool for a couple of minutes before pouring in the filling. Refrigerate for at least 6-8 hours or until set up. Serve and enjoy!

Nutrition Facts

Amounts per Serving

Calories: 359 Kcal | Fat: 42.5g | Carbs: 5.1g | Protein: 6.5g

Peppermint Cheesecake Pie

Preparation time: 30 minutes

Servings: 12 slices

Ingredients:

Crust:

- 2 cups of sunflower seeds or almond meal
- 1/3 cup of unsweetened cocoa powder
- 4 tablespoons of butter, melted
- ¼ teaspoon of salt
- ¼ cup of Swerve sweetener

Filling:

- 16 oz. of cream cheese room temperature
- 1 teaspoon of peppermint liquid stevia
- 1 teaspoon of peppermint extract
- ¼ teaspoon of salt
- 1 cup of heavy cream

Topping:

- ½ cup of heavy cream
- ½ teaspoon of peppermint liquid stevia
- ¼ teaspoon of peppermint extract
- ½ cup of sugar-free candy canes crushed

Cooking Instructions:

1. In a food processor, add together all the no-bake ingredients to make the crust. Blend the ingredients until the mix is a fine crumb consistency.

2. Taste and adjust the crust taste by adding more sweetener. Spread the mixture into a 9-inch pie dish. Set aside.

3. In a stand mixer, add together all the filling ingredients, except heavy cream and blend on high until smooth. Taste and add more stevia. Pour in heavy cream.

4. Blend on high until all is incorporated. Spread the mixture over the pie crust. In a stand mixer, add together all of the topping ingredients except crushed candy canes, if desired.

5. Blend on high until whipped. Taste and adjust stevia, if desired. Spread this over the cheesecake filling. Refrigerate pie for at least 3-4 hours.

6. Serve and enjoy!

Nutrition Facts

Amount per Serving

Calories: 344 Kcal | Fat: 33.4g | Carbohydrates: 5.1g | Protein: 5.3g

Grasshopper Pie

Preparation time: 15 minutes

Cook time: 0 minutes

Servings: 12 slices

Ingredients:

Brownie Crust:

- 1 ½ cup of walnuts
- 7 medjool dates pitted
- 1/3 cup of cacao
- 1 teaspoon of vanilla
- 1/8 teaspoon of pink salt

Mint Cream Filling:

- 2 cups of raw cashews, soaked
- 1 tightly packed cup baby spinach
- ½ cup of maple syrup
- 2/3 cup of coconut oil, melted
- 1 tablespoon of vanilla
- 2 teaspoons of mint extract
- Dash of pink salt

Cooking Instructions:

1. Line a baking sheet with parchment paper. In a food processor, blend together all the crust ingredients until a sticky dough forms. Press crust evenly into a pie plate.

2. Ensure that cashews have been soaked overnight or at least 2 hours. Drain the cashew, rinse and shake dry.

3. Blend cashews and spinach in a food processor until broken down. Scrape down sides and add the rest of the ingredients. Blend the ingredients again.

4. Taste and adjust the taste for sweetness. Pour the mixture over crust, and flatten the top with a spatula. Cover and refrigerate for about 2 hours or until set.

5. Garnish with chocolate shavings or cacao nibs, if desired. Serve and enjoy!!

Almond Flour Pie

Preparation time: 5 minutes

Cook time: 10 minutes

Total time: 15 minutes

Serves: 12 Slices

Ingredients:

- 2 ½ cup of Blanched almond flour
- 1/3 cup of Erythritol (or your desired sweetener)
- ¼ teaspoon of Sea salt
- 1 cup of Ghee (solid, then melted)
- 1 large Egg (or 2 tablespoons of additional ghee)
- ½ teaspoon of vanilla extract, optional

Cooking Instructions:

1. Preheat the oven to 350°F / 177°C. Cover the bottom of a 9 inch round pie pan with parchment paper or spray with cooking spray.

2. In a medium bowl, combine together the almond flour, erythritol (if desired), and sea salt. Stir in the melted ghee and egg, and give everything a good stir to combine.

3. If using vanilla, stir the vanilla into the melted ghee before adding to the dry ingredients. Press and stir the dough until there is no almond flour powder left.

4. Press the dough into the bottom of the prepared pan. Carefully poke holes in the surface with a fork to avoid bubbling.

5. Place in the oven. Bake for 10-12 minutes, or until lightly golden. Allow to cool for a couple of minutes. Serve and enjoy!

Nutrition Facts

Amount per Serving

Calories: 180 Kcal | Fat: 17g | Protein: 6g | Total Carbs: 5g

Graham Cracker Pie

Preparation time: 20 minutes

Chilling time: 1 hour

Total Time: 20 minutes

Servings: 1

Ingredients:

For 'Graham Cracker' Crust:

- 25 g almond flour
- 2-3 tsp. of powdered erythritol or xylitol
- 1/8 tsp. of ground cinnamon
- Dash of kosher salt
- 2-3 tsp. of melted grass-fed butter as desired

Cooking Instructions:

1. Lightly toast almond flour in a pan over medium heat for about 4 minutes or until golden and fragrant.

2. Transfer toasted almond flour to a medium bowl. Stir in sweetener, cinnamon and salt.

3. Add in butter, and give everything a good mix to combine. Press in to the pie dish.

4. Refrigerate while you make the filling. Serve and enjoy!

Nutrition Facts

Amount per Serving

Calories: 213 Kcal | Total Fat: 20g | Total Carbohydrates: 5g | Protein 5g

FROZEN DESSERTS

Mint and Chocolate Chip Ice Bombs

Yields: 14 ice bombs

Ingredients:

- 1 medium ripe avocado, halved, pitted, and peeled
- 1 cup of full-fat mascarpone cheese or creamed coconut milk
- ¼ cup plus 1 tablespoon of powdered Erythritol or Swerve
- 1 teaspoon of peppermint extract, or 1 tablespoon of fresh mint
- Few drops liquid stevia, optional
- 2.1 ounces of dark chocolate, chopped

Cooking Instructions:

1. In a food processor, combine together the avocado flesh, mascarpone or creamed coconut milk, erythritol or Swerve, and mint extract or fresh mint.

2. Add few drops of stevia if you desire a sweeter taste. Blend the ingredients until smooth. Mix in the chopped dark chocolate.

3. Add about 2 tbsp. of the mixture into each of 14 small silicone muffin mots or candy molds, or round cake pop molds.

4. Refrigerate for at least 2 hours or until set. Serve and enjoy!

Strawberry-Basil Ice Cups

Yields: 10 ice cups

Ingredients:

- ½ cup of creamed coconut milk, at room temperature
- ¾ cup of cream cheese or creamed coconut milk, at room temperature
- ¼ cup of powdered erythritol or Swerve
- ¼ cup of unsalted butter or coconut oil, at room temperature
- 1 teaspoon of sugar-free vanilla extract, or ½ teaspoon of vanilla powder
- Few drops liquid stevia, optional
- 1 cup of fresh strawberries
- 2 tbsp. of fresh basil leaves

Cooking Instructions:

1. Add together the creamed coconut milk, cream cheese or more creamed coconut milk, erythritol or Swerve, and butter in a food processor.

2. Add the coconut oil, and vanilla. Blend the ingredients until smooth and creamy. Add the stevia if you want a sweeter taste and pulse again.

3. Divide the mixture from the processor into half and set aside. Add about ¾ cup of strawberries to the remaining mixture in the processor

4. Pulse until smooth. Slice the rest of the ¼ cup of strawberries and set aside for topping. Divide the strawberry cream cheese mixture into 10 silicone muffin cups.

5. Combine the other half of the cream cheese with the basil in a food processor. Pulse until smooth. Top each cup with 1 ½ tbsp. of the basil mixture.

6. Finish each with a few strawberry slices. Refrigerate for at least 2 hours, or until set. Serve and enjoy!

Vanilla Ice Cream

Preparation time: 30 minutes

Cook time: 15 minutes

Total time: 45 minutes

Servings: 8

Ingredients:

- 1 recipe Sugar-Free Condensed Milk
- 1 ½ cups of heavy cream
- 3 tablespoons of powdered Swerve Sweetener
- 1 ½ tablespoon of vodka, optional
- ½ teaspoon of vanilla extract
- 1/8 teaspoon of salt

Cooking Instructions:

1. Make the sweetened condensed milk according to the directions. Allow the condensed milk to cool to room temperature.

2. Add together the heavy cream, powdered sweetener, vodka, vanilla extract, and salt. Give everything a good whisk. Taste and adjust sweetener to taste.

3. Refrigerate for at least 1 hour or overnight. Add into the canister of an ice cream maker and churn according to manufacturer's directions.

4. Transfer to an airtight container and refrigerate for at least 4 hours or until set. Serve and enjoy!

Nutrition Facts

Amount per Serving

Calories: 319 Kcal | Total Fat: 31.4g | Total Carbohydrates: 2.4g | Protein: 1.7g

Shamrock Shake

Preparation time: 5 minutes

Cook time: 0 minutes

Total time: 5 minutes

Yield: 1 shake

Ingredients:

- ½ medium avocado
- 1 scoop of dairy free vanilla protein powder
- ½ cup of Silk Almond Coconut Milk
- 8 ice cubes
- 1/8 tsp. of peppermint extract
- 5 drops natural green food coloring, optional
- 2 tbsp. of coconut milk whipped cream, optional
- 1 tbsp. of sugar-free dark chocolate chips

Cooking Instructions:

1. In a blender, combine together the avocado, protein powder, almond coconut milk, ice, peppermint extract and food coloring.

2. Blend the ingredients until blended and creamy. Top with dairy free whipped cream and sugar-free chocolate chips, if desired.

3. Serve and enjoy!

Nutrition Facts

Amounts per Serving

Calories: 259 Kcal | Fat: 14g | Carbohydrates: 7g | Protein: 26g

Peanut Butter Chocolate Ice Cream

Preparation time: 30 minutes

Cook time: 30 minutes

Total time: 1 hour

Servings: 8

Ingredients:

- 2 packets Frappaketo Chocolate Peanut Butter Cream
- 1 cup of Unsweetened Almond milk or Coconut Milk
- 1.5 cups of Heavy Cream or Coconut Cream, if desired
- 2 tablespoons of Powdered Monk Fruit Erythritol
- 1 tablespoon of Honest Syrup Caramel or Maple
- 2 tablespoons of Salted Butter
- ¼ teaspoon of Xanthan Gum

Cooking Instructions:

1. In a medium bowl, whisk together the Frappaketo with the almond milk and set aside. Whisk the heavy cream, powdered erythritol, and honest syrup.

2. Pour the combined mixture to a saucepan and heat on medium-low heat until bubbling. Turn the pan on low heat for about 30 minutes.

3. Remove the pan from the heat and sprinkle with the Xanthan Gum. Give everything a good mix to incorporate the Xanthan Gum.

4. Allow to rest for about 10-15 minutes. Add the heavy cream mixture to the Frappaketo mixture.

5. Add them to the ice cream maker and churn on the "Ice Cream" setting. Serve and enjoy!

Nutrition Facts

Amount per Serving

Calories: 257 Kcal | Total Fat: 27g | Total Carbohydrates: 5g | Protein 4g

Butter Pecan Ice Cream

Servings: 8

Ingredients:

- ¼ cup of butter
- 2 cups of heavy cream
- ½ cup of Swerve sweetener confectioners
- ¼ teaspoon of salt
- 2 egg yolks
- 2 teaspoons of maple extract
- 1 tablespoon of Choczero Maple Pecan sweetener or your desired sweetener
- 1 tablespoon of MCT oil
- 2 tablespoons of pecans toasted, chopped

Cooking Instructions:

1. Dissolve the butter in small sauce pan. Add together the heavy cream, Swerve sweetener and salt. Heat over low heat.

2. Whisk egg yolks until light in color. Add 1 tbsp. of the butter cream mixture and stir into the yolks. Continue with a few more spoonfuls into the yolks.

3. Slowly add the rest of the yolk into the mixture on the stove. Give everything a good stir until mixture thickens over low heat and coats the back of a spoon, 175°F.

4. Pour into a bowl and refrigerate for about 30 minutes. Add together the maple extract and Choczero sweetener or your desired sweetener and MCT oil.

5. Give everything a good stir to combine. Pour mixture into your ice cream machine. Follow manufacturer's instructions.

6. Stir in pecans, spread ice cream into an 8 by 5 loaf pan and refrigerate for at least 2-3 hours or until soft. Serve and enjoy!

Nutrition Facts

Amount per Serving

Calories: 302 Kcal | Total Fat: 32g | Total Carbohydrates: 2g | Protein: 2g

Peanut Butter Cup Milkshake

Yield: 2

Ingredients:

- 2 scoops Ketologie Chocolate Keto Shake
- 3 tablespoons of Swerve Confectioners
- 1 cup of coconut cream
- 1 cup of heavy cream
- 2 cups of ice
- 3 tablespoons of crunchy peanut butter or Legendary Foods Peanut Butter Chocolate Chip Sugar-free Nut Butter
- 2 tablespoons or 1 shot of rum, optional
- Choc Zero Chocolate Honest Syrup for drizzling, optional

Cooking Instructions:

1. In a high-speed blender, add together all of the ingredients.

2. Pulse the ingredients on high speed until smooth.

3. Serve and enjoy!

Strawberry Homemade Ice Cream

Preparation time: 5 minutes

Freeze: 2 hours

Total time: 5 minutes

Servings: 3

Ingredients:

- 1 cup of heavy cream
- 1 cup of strawberries, diced
- 1 tsp. of vanilla
- 1 tsp. of Liquid Stevia

Cooking Instructions:

1. Pour Heavy cream into Mason jar. Add strawberries and vanilla. Add the Liquid Stevia to Mason jar.

2. Seal the lid tight on Mason jar and shake very well for about 5 minutes. Leave top on Mason jar and refrigerate for at least 2-3 hours.

3. Serve and enjoy!

Nutrition Facts

Amounts per Serving

Calories: 292kcal | Carbohydrates: 6g | Protein: 1g | Fat: 29g

MOUSSE & CUSTARD

Chocolate Mousse

Servings: 6

Ingredients:

- 1¼ cups of heavy whipping cream
- ½ teaspoon of vanilla extract
- 2 egg yolks
- A pinch salt
- 3 ounces of dark chocolate with a minimum of 80% cocoa solids, break into small pieces

Cooking Instructions:

1. Melt the dark chocolate in the microwave for 20-second intervals, stirring constantly. Keep aside at room temperature.

2. In a medium bowl, whip the cream to soft peaks and add the vanilla. In a different bowl, mix egg yolks with salt.

3. Add the melted chocolate to the egg yolks and give everything a good mix to form a smooth batter. Add a few spoonful's of whipped cream to the chocolate mix.

4. Give everything a good stir. Add the rest of the cream and fold it through. Divide the batter into ramekins.

5. Place in the fridge to chill for at least 2 hours. Serve with fresh berries, if desired and enjoy!

Peanut Butter Mousse

Preparation time: 5 minutes

Total time: 5 minutes

Servings: 4

Ingredients:

- ½ cup of heavy whipping cream
- 4 ounces of cream cheese, softened
- ¼ cup of natural peanut butter
- ¼ cup of powdered Swerve Sweetener
- ½ teaspoon of vanilla extract

Cooking Instructions:

1. Whip the ½ cup of cream in a large bowl and set aside. In a separate bowl, beat together the cream cheese and peanut butter until smooth.

2. Add together the sweetener and vanilla. Add a pinch of salt and beat until smooth. Add 2 tablespoons of heavy cream if your mixture is too thick.

3. Beat everything until combined. Fold in the whipped cream until no streaks remain. Ladle into little dessert glasses.

4. Drizzle with a little low carb chocolate sauce, if desired. Serve and enjoy!

Nutrition Facts

Amount per Serving

Calories: 301 Kcal | Total Fat: 26.5g | Total Carbohydrates: 5.6g | Protein 5.9g

Vanilla Custard

Preparation time: 15 minutes

Cook time: 5 minutes

Total time: 20 minutes

Servings: 5

Ingredients:

- 2 cups of Pure Cream or whipping heavy cream
- 6 large Egg yolks
- 2 tablespoons of Granulated Sweetener
- 1 Vanilla Bean or 2 teaspoons of vanilla extract
- A pinch of Salt

Cooking Instructions:

1. Slice the vanilla bean in half and remove out the seeds. In a small saucepan, add together the vanilla bean, seeds, salt and cream.

2. Heat over medium heat, stirring frequently until just boiling. Remove the saucepan from heat. In a medium bowl, whisk together the egg yolks and sweetener to combine.

3. Pour the hot cream mixture over the egg yolks, whisking constantly. Add the mixture to a clean saucepan.

4. Cook over medium-low heat, stirring constantly until thickened. Remove from the heat and strain to remove the vanilla pod.

5. Serve and enjoy!

Nutrition Facts

Amounts per Serving

Calories: 400kcal | Carbohydrates: 3g | Protein: 5g | Fat: 41g

Crème Anglaise Custard

Preparation time: 15 minutes

Cook time: 5 minutes

Total time: 20 minutes

Serves: 4

Ingredients:

- 3 extra large egg yolks
- 300g double cream
- 2 tablespoons of Sukrin icing 'sugar'
- 1 vanilla pod or 1 teaspoon of vanilla paste
- A pinch of fine Himalayan pink salt

Cooking Instructions:

1. Whip together the egg yolks with icing 'sugar' and salt using an electric whip until foamy. Add together the cream and vanilla seeds in a small saucepan.

2. Heat the cream, stirring, until just boiling. Add the hot cream into the whipped yolks and give everything a good whisk.

3. Return the crème anglaise back to the saucepan cream and cook on medium heat. Continue whisking, while you boil.

4. Once it thickens, remove from heat. Serve with your desired dessert.

Nutrition Facts

Amounts per Serving

Calories: 380 | Fat: 40g | Carbs: 1.3g | Protein: 3.7g

Caramel Mousse

Preparation time: 10 minutes

Total time: 10 minutes

Servings: 1

Ingredients:

- 1 (1.64 oz.) serving Keto Chow Salted Caramel Ultra-Low Carbohydrate Meal Replacement Shake Mix
- ¼ cup of water
- ¼ cup of organic heavy whipping cream, whipped
- 2 Chocoperfection Dark European Chocolate mini bars (about 2 tbsp.), chopped

Cooking Instructions:

1. In a medium bowl, stir together the shake mix and water until smooth.

2. Fold in the whipped cream and chill in the fridge for at least 30 to 45 minutes, stirring every 10 minutes.

3. Top with the chocolate, if desired. Serve and enjoy!

Nutrition Facts

Amount per Serving

Calories: 368 Kcal | Total Fat: 26g | Total Carbohydrates: 13g | Protein: 27g

Chocolate Custard

Preparation time: 5 minutes

Total time: 35 minutes

Servings: 4

Ingredients:

- ½ cup of whole milk or unsweetened soy milk
- 3 large eggs
- 3 ½ oz. of dark chocolate (at least 70% cacao), broken into small pieces
- 1 medium peach, pitted and sliced, or about 1 cup other seasonal fruit, for garnish

Cooking Instructions:

1. In a small saucepan, heat the milk over medium heat, stirring constantly until bubbling. Remove the milk from heat.

2. In a medium bowl, whisk the eggs and set aside. Dissolve the chocolate in a double boiler, then remove from the heat.

3. While whisking, gently pour milk about 3 tbsp. at a time to the melted chocolate, whisking until you have added all the milk.

4. Gently add the whisked eggs to the dissolve chocolate mixture while whisking continuously. Return back on the double boiler.

5. Cook, stirring constantly for about 5 minutes or until the mixture thickens. Remove from the heat. Divide the mixture into four small ramekins.

6. Place in the fridge and chill for at least 20 minutes or until fully cooled. Garnish with peach slices.

7. Serve and enjoy!

Pumpkin Cheesecake Mousse

Preparation time: 5 minutes

Total time: 5 minutes

Servings: 12

Ingredients:

- 16 oz. of cream cheese, room temperature
- 15 oz. of canned pumpkin
- 2 cups of heavy cream
- ¼ teaspoon of salt
- 2 tsp. of pumpkin pie spice or use cinnamon, ginger, nutmeg, cloves
- 1-2 tsp. of Pumpkin Spice liquid stevia or Vanilla Stevia
- 1 tsp. of vanilla extract
- Sukrin Gold Brown Sugar Substitute, optional for topping

Cooking Instructions:

1. In a stand mixer, blend together the cream cheese and pumpkin until smooth. Add the remaining ingredients and blend for about 5 minutes or until fluffy.

2. Taste and adjust sweetener to suit your desired taste. Pour the mixture into serving glasses. Top with cacao nibs or brown sugar sub like Sukrin if needed.

3. Refrigerate for at least 1 hour. Keep refrigerated until ready to serve. Serve and enjoy!

Nutrition Facts

Amount per Serving

Calories: 280 Kcal | Total Fat: 27g | Total Carbohydrates: 5g | Protein: 3g

Almond Milk Custard

Preparation time: 2 minutes

Cook time: 5-10 minutes

Servings: 2

Ingredients:

- 1 egg
- 1 tbsp. of tapioca starch (arrowroot) or corn starch
- 1 tbsp. of maple syrup
- 1 cup of almond milk
- 1 tbsp. of cacao powder, for chocolate custard
- Add a large piece of orange or lemon rind to the mixture, add for citrus custard during cooking
- Add 1 split vanilla bean or add 1 tsp. of vanilla extract, add for vanilla custard during cooking

Cooking Instructions:

1. In a medium bowl, whisk together the egg, starch and sweetener until smooth. Slowly pour the almond milk, and ensure that it forms a smooth texture.

2. Heat on the stove for about, whisking constantly until the mixture thickens for about 5 minutes.

3. Remove from heat. Serve immediately and enjoy!

Nutrition Facts

Amounts per Serving

Calories: 89 Kcal | Total Fat: 4g | Carbohydrate: 11g | Protein: 4g

Egg Custard

Preparation time: 5 minutes

Cook time: 30 minutes

Total time: 35 minutes

Servings: 6

Ingredients:

- 3 large eggs
- 2 cups of heavy whipping cream
- ¼ cup of Swerve or granulated sweetener
- 1 tbsp. of vanilla
- ½ tsp. of ground cinnamon, optional
- ¼ tsp. of salt

Cooking Instructions:

1. Preheat the oven to 350°F. Bring a kettle of water to boil. In a medium bowl, beat the eggs until light yellow and foamy.

2. Mix in cinnamon. Add together the sweetener, cream, salt and vanilla and give everything a good mix.

3. Fill the custard cups with the custard mixture and transfer the custard cups in a cake pan or large casserole.

4. Fill the dish with a few drops of hot water surrounding the custard cups. Place the custard in the oven and bake at 350°F for 30 minutes, or until firm in the middle.

5. Serve warm or cold. If you are serving it cold, then place in the fridge for at least 2-3 hours before serving.

Nutrition Facts

Amounts per Serving

Calories: 319 Kcal | Fat: 32g | Carbohydrates: 3g | Protein: 5g

Pumpkin Custard

Preparation time: 5 minutes

Cook time: 40 minutes

Total time: 45 minutes

Servings: 6

Ingredients:

- 15 oz. of pumpkin puree 425g
- 1 tsp. of liquid monk fruit sweetener or liquid stevia
- 1 tsp. of cinnamon
- ¼ tsp. of ginger
- 1/8 tsp. of cloves
- 4 large egg yolks
- ¾ cup of coconut cream

Cooking Instructions:

1. Preheat the oven to 350°F. In a medium bowl, combine together the pumpkin, sweetener, cinnamon, ginger, and cloves.

2. Beat in egg yolks until incorporated. Stir in the coconut cream and spoon the mixture into individual ramekins.

3. Place in the oven and bake at 350°F for 30-40 minutes or until firm. Place on a wire rack to cool. Refrigerate for at least 4 hours.

4. Serve and enjoy!

Nutrition Facts

Amount per Serving

Calories: 160 Kcal | Total Fat: 13g | Total Carbohydrates: 8g | Protein: 3g

CANDY & CONFECTIONS

Chocolate Coconut Fat Bombs

Servings: 6

Ingredients:

- 10-20 mg CBD oil. about 1-2 full droppers
- ½ cup of coconut butter
- ½ cup of raw cacao powder
- ½ cup of coconut oil
- 1 tsp. of raw honey, birch xylitol or MitoSweet, optional

Cooking Instructions:

1. Melt the coconut oil in a saucepan on low heat. Whisk in cacao powder until there's no more lumps. Add sweetener (if desired), and stir again until dissolved.

2. Pour the cacao mixture into 6 cups using a silicone muffin pan. Chill for at least 30 minutes, or until chocolate mixture is set.

3. Melt the coconut butter in a saucepan on low heat. Remove from heat and whisk in CBD oil. Remove muffin mold from the refrigerator.

4. Add the coconut butter mixture to the top of each cup. Refrigerate for another 30 minutes or until set. Store fat bombs in the refrigerator.

5. Serve and enjoy!

Nutritional Facts

Amounts per Serving

Calories: 324 Kcal | Protein: 3g | Carbs: 10.6g | Fat: 31.8g

Butterscotch Candy

Servings: 16

Cook time: 20 minutes

Total time: 20 minutes

Ingredients:

- 1 cup of butter
- ½ cup of Lakanto Golden Monkfruit Sweetener
- 1 teaspoon of vanilla extract
- 1 teaspoon of pink Himalayan salt

Cooking Instructions:

1. Melt the butter in a saucepan over medium heat. Once butter has melted, add the sweetener and stir constantly. Bring the mixture a low boil, stirring constantly.

2. Reduce the heat and stir until mixture is a nice. Remove from heat and stir in vanilla and salt. Allow to cool for about 3 minutes, stirring occasionally.

3. Pour into an 8 x 8 glass storage container. Refrigerate overnight, or for at least 8 hours to be firm.

4. Serve and enjoy!

Nutrition Facts

Amount per Serving

Calories: 102 Kcal | Total Fat: 12g | Carbohydrates: 0g | Protein: 0g

Lemon Drop Gummies

Preparation time: 15 minutes

Cook time: 15 minutes

Servings: 4

Ingredients:

- ¼ cup of fresh lemon juice
- 1 tbsp. of water
- 2 tbsp. of gelatin powder
- 2 tbsp. of erythritol or stevia, to taste

Cooking Instructions:

1. Heat the lemon juice and water in a small saucepan.
2. Slowly stir in the gelatin powder and erythritol to dissolve.
3. Pour into silicone molds and refrigerate for at least 2 hours.
4. Serve and enjoy!

Nutrition Facts

Amounts per Serving

Calories: 15 Kcal | Fat: 0 g | Carbohydrates: 1 g | Protein: 3 g

Vanilla Fat Bombs

Preparation time: 10 minutes

Cook time: 0 minutes

Servings: 16

Ingredients:

- 1 cup coconut butter
- 1 cup coconut milk
- 1 cup unsweetened shredded coconut
- 1 Tablespoon vanilla extract
- Stevia to taste
- ¼ cup 100% dark chocolate

Cooking Instructions:

1. In a saucepan, add together the coconut butter and coconut milk and melt over low heat. Add all the remaining ingredients except for the dark chocolate.

2. Give everything a good mix. Transfer the mixture to chill in the refrigerator for at least 2 hours.

3. Form small balls from the mixture and add the balls into the fridge to solidify for 2-3 hours. Melt the dark chocolate in the microwave.

4. Dip each of the balls into the chocolate, and place the dipped balls onto parchment paper. Transfer back to the refrigerator to chill until set.

5. Serve and enjoy!

Nutrition Facts

Amounts per Serving

Calories: 180 Kcal | Fat: 16 g | Carbohydrates: 5 g | Protein: 3 g

Peppermint Frost Breath Mints

Ingredients:

- 1 Cup of xylitol
- 4 Drops peppermint extract

Cooking Instructions:

1. In a pan over low heat, add the xylitol to melt.
2. Allow to cool and add the peppermint oil.
3. Spread on parchment and dry thoroughly for at least 24 hours.
4. Serve and enjoy!

Lemon Curd

Preparation time: 10 minutes

Cook time: 10 minutes

Total time: 20 minutes

Servings: 4

Ingredients:

- 4 Lemons (Juice and Zest)
- ½ Cup of Natvia (Or Erythritol)
- 100 g of Butter
- 3 Whole Eggs
- 1 Egg Yolk

Cooking Instructions:

1. In a medium heatproof bowl, squeeze the lemons, and zest the skin. Add together the natvia (or erythritol) and butter.

2. Place the heatproof bowl over a pan of slowly simmering water. Stir the mixture until all the butter has melted.

3. Whisk the eggs and egg yolk. Stir into the heated mixture and give everything a good stir. Cook for about 10 minutes or until the mixture coats the back of a spoon.

4. Remove from the heat and add the mixture into sterilized jars. Store in the refrigerator for at least 2 weeks.

5. Serve and enjoy!

Nutrition Facts

Amount per Serving

Calories: 258 Kcal | Carbohydrates: 2g | Protein: 7g | Fat: 25g

www.ingramcontent.com/pod-product-compliance
Lightning Source LLC
Chambersburg PA
CBHW051807100526
44592CB00016B/2596